The Legend
1927-2015

BART

A Tribute

During his remarkable career, Bart Cummings trained 268 Group 1 winners (listed here), from Stormy Passage, in the 1958 SA Derby, to the last, Hallowed Crown in March 2015 in the Randwick Guineas. Along the journey he trained 1265 Stakes winners with an amazing 45 Stakes races in the 1974-75 season.

A glorious life

This remarkable photo describes only part of the huge tapestry that was the life of Bart Cummings. That he trained 12 Melbourne Cup winners is not only racing's greatest legend, and one that will never be equalled, but what's more important he will always be an integral part of the Australian story.

His long-serving Melbourne foreman and friend, Reg Fleming said of his boss: "There's Bradman, and there's Bart, and that's how it is." Each of them grew up without privilege; each was self-taught, although Cummings did attribute some of his knowledge to his father: "Dad was a strict man. I was always getting orders from him, but things he told me I remember and use."

Bart's son, Anthony, announced the death of his father on Twitter, a form of communication that may have developed its limit of 140 characters per tweet from Bart's quipped responses to any of the thousands of questions he parried through more than 60 years of training racehorses. Anthony put in stone an obituary all of us would enjoy: "He lived a full life."

That life was devoted to family and racing. Anthony, a successful trainer in his own right, also pointed out that just two days before his passing, Bart had celebrated his 61st wedding anniversary with Valmae, whom Bart had described cheekily back in 1974, after 20 years of marriage: "Like a good filly, she caught my eye."

Cups and quips: that was how most of us knew Bart, and it was always just Bart. So often the headlines on the morning papers across the country on those first Wednesdays in November

would cry out: "Bart does it again" or "Cup number (fill in two to 12) for Bart".

But this tribute to Bart is not just about Cups or Group 1 wins, or about the array of great champions he produced, it's about contribution, a contribution to the sport that transcended winning and losing. Bart may have kept his media responses brief, but he was always available, always there to promote his runners, and by extension the sport that he loved; he drew smart media types to him like those famous flies in his Glenelg stable ("How many can I have?" he asked the health inspector, when told he had too many flies in his stables).

He was hard to know. The great storyteller, Les Carlyon, who tracked his career from his earliest moments of fame to its gentle finale described him as "unknowable" in his obituary, but those who were close to him knew that Bart remained loyal to himself and the methods that had worked for him through generations of change. "The cheapest thing in racing," he often said, "is patience and it's the most seldom used, so I did it the cheap way—plenty of time and patience and it's paid off for me handsomely". But such a quick grab of his philosophy downplays the need to choose the stock wisely, as Fleming noted: "He had a great eye for horses. I saw the horses that came through and they were great looking horses. Some weren't great looking horses when they came in but in 12 months' time you could see what he saw before that. He was just…" He never finished that line, but we all knew what was to come. He was just…Bart.

—*Geoff Slattery*

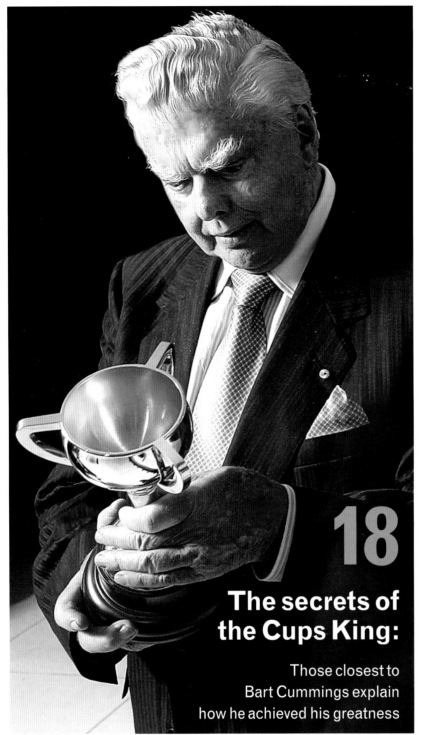

18

The secrets of the Cups King:

Those closest to
Bart Cummings explain
how he achieved his greatness

BART
The Legend

© The Slattery Media Group Pty Ltd, 2015

First published by The Slattery Media Group Pty Ltd
in October 2015

All images reproduced with permission.

All rights reserved. No part of this publication may be
reproduced, stored in any retrieval system or transmitted
in any form by any means without prior permission of the
copyright owner. Inquiries should be made to the publisher.

ISBN: 978-0-9873428-0-5

The Slattery Media Group Pty Ltd,
1 Albert Street, Richmond,
Victoria, Australia, 3121

Visit slatterymedia.com

Group Publisher and Editor
Geoff Slattery

Publications Manager:
Courtney Nicholls

Contributors:
Geoff Slattery, Joe McGrath, Stephen Moran,
Danny Power, Stephen Howell, Adrian Dunn

Designers:
Chris Downey and Kate Slattery

Printed by Graphic Impressions Australia

Cover:
A familiar smiling face on race days through more than
60 years of training racehorses. Bart Cummings was a
winner—the trainer of 268 G1 winners, and 1265 Stakes
Winners. He truly was Australia's greatest horse trainer.
(Herald and Weekly Times)

The Slattery Media Group thanks the Herald & Weekly Times
Pty Ltd for its kind support of this publication.

The photographs included in this publication are reproduced
under, inter alia, licence from the Herald & Weekly Times
Pty Limited, News Limited and its subsidiary related bodies
corporate and are protected by the Copyright Laws of
Australia. All rights are reserved. Other than for the purposes
and subject to the conditions under the Copyright Laws,
no photograph may be reproduced, stored in a retrieval
system, or transmitted in any form or by any means,
electronic, mechanical, photocopying, recording, or otherwise
without the prior express written permission of the Herald
& Weekly Times Pty Ltd, News Limited and its subsidiary
related subsidiary companies.

All photos supplied by the Herald & Weekly Times
unless otherwise marked.

slattery MEDIA GROUP **Herald Sun**

RELAXING:
Enjoying the fruits of his labours, with the 1999 Melbourne Cup trophy at his feet, Bart Cummings is more than likely looking ahead to the following year. As he often said, it's the future that counts, while learning from the past.

The freakish, amazing titan of the turf

JOE MCGRATH recalls with a smile the dry, deadpan responses to interviewers' questions and how Bart Cummings, the man the VRC was grateful to have called a friend, never gave much away—except, that is, his time and energy to promote the racing game.

What do you say about Bart? A champion. A man ahead of his time. A visionary and a master horseman. A freak. He was all of those things and more. He broke records, set new ones and then shattered those as well, doing more for racing and the Melbourne Cup brand than any other individual. In total, he would train near 7000 winners, of which 268 were at Group 1 level, if you include the pair he co-trained with grandson James. In doing all this, he established a profile hailed at racetracks throughout the world and a reputation that will never fade. Everyone knew who Bart Cummings was.

It has been said that Bart was to racing what Bradman was to cricket; a master of his craft in an industry where competition positions itself on a knife's edge and luck is a key factor. That said, some are luckier than others.

To provide a home truth, I was born about six months before the first of Bart's 12 Cup wins in 1965. By the time I reached 10 he had trained five Melbourne Cup winners, equaling the record set by Etienne de Mestre 100 years earlier and putting himself ahead of John Tait, Walter Hickenbotham, Richard Bradfield and James Scobie, each with four Cups. He was already a legend before I was out of short pants, already a figure of such awesome achievement that I labored for a while under a child's misconception that Bart always won the Melbourne Cup! Being brought up in a racing

family, I understood quickly the importance of the Cup to the nation. Bart was a glorious extension of the Cup story. He was such a regular fixture with the Cup in the 1970s, God only knows what inner force sustained him to win 12 of them into the new century.

Actually, come to think of it, I did hear him say one day there was one particular motivator. While the VRC was compiling the 150th Melbourne Cup DVD, *The Story of the Melbourne Cup: Australia's Greatest Race* in 2010, Bart was grilled by the Seven network's talented sports commentator Neil Kearney as to what drove him each year to keep climbing the mountain. Typically deadpan, he replied, 'Prizemoney!' Not entirely happy with the answer and looking for another angle, Neil cleverly posed the question once again in a different form, hoping for a different result. You guessed it, same answer. This time, even more deadpan, 'Prizemoney!' But that was Bart. He wasn't going to let you know exactly what made him tick, but he made sure to give you a few teasers along the way. His 'answers', such as they were, came wrapped in that trademark dry humour.

My recollections of Bart are varied. In later years they would focus predominantly on the promotion of the Emirates Melbourne Cup Tour. Started in 2003, the year that saw Makybe Diva collect the first of her three Cups, the tour is centred on taking 'The People's Cup' back to the people. It has been a successful marketing initiative by telling the story of the Melbourne Cup and giving people the opportunity to meet

the race's heroes and actually hold the Cup, just as the winners have done and will continue doing as long as this great race is run. As Bart knew, not many get to touch it, especially on Melbourne Cup Day.

Before the 2003 tour, I had met Bart several times, but when it came to promoting the Cup Tour and the Spring Carnival he would become a central player in delivering the message. He was certainly key in the celebration of the 150th Melbourne Cup in 2010. While he had always been professional in his approach, it was during this time that I also saw the generous side of Bart, always willing to assist in the marketing and promotion of the carnival. Even if he wasn't too sure why we were doing what we were doing and what we wanted him to do, he would do it anyway. He liked the Victoria Racing Club; liked Flemington even more, and he *loved the Melbourne Cup.*

I have thought much of what might have been since his passing. Had he elected to focus on the Golden Slipper Stakes in Sydney with as much passion and focus as he brought to Flemington, maybe this story would have a different twist. We can be thankful that he strapped the mighty Comic Court at the 1950 Melbourne Cup, when he was captivated by the atmosphere and vowed one day to come back and win his own.

In first engaging Bart in promotional activities, you would go through his office at Leilani Lodge in Sydney and be directed to Bill Charles, his racing manager. Bill, a great guy, was always willing to help your cause where and when he could. I recall one occasion when I was organising the 'Homecoming of the Cup' function at the Sofitel in Melbourne. It was eight days out from the 2009 race and we had been targeting international talent to feature on the night. As with these sort of functions, there is always a bit of running around before your talent is lined up and locked down. On this occasion, just when we thought we had our talent all parcelled up, the stars pulled out (for whatever reasons).

When Plan A fails you go to Plan B; when Plan B falls over there is, of course, Plan C. By this stage, however, we were looking at Plan D! Frustrated, I thought we would go to Plan A+. Who is the biggest name in the business? Who pulls more people to racing events, and who is synonymous with the Cup Carnival? Of course it was Bart Cummings. After I pitched the idea to Bill Charles, he rang back to say, 'Well, he didn't say 'no', which is always a good thing to hear. He said, 'Ring back at midday on his mobile. You might be a chance.' That I did. I told Bart what the function was about and promised we would pick him up with his wife, Valmae, from Melbourne's Crown Hotel. He said, 'That would

be good'. And then I said, '...and we will drop you home.' He said, 'Even better!'

As it turned out, Viewed won the Caulfield Cup three days after we had locked him in. So You Think won the Cox Plate the following Saturday and, like a flash, Bart was once again on the front page of every paper across the country, just like so many times before. His involvement on the night was a roaring success, with him enjoying rock star status. I had learned a valuable lesson: when Plan A fails, don't go to lesser options. Go straight to Plan A+.

Bart's wit was refreshing in the serious world of horse racing. On one occasion I rang to explain that the Victoria Racing Club (VRC) would be presenting him with three miniature Melbourne

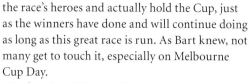

" Bart was always willing to assist in the promotion of the carnival. Even if he wasn't too sure why we were doing what we were doing, he would do it anyway. "

Cups. At the time the VRC, under the direction of chairman Rod Fitzroy, elected to honour all winning trainers and jockeys between 1919 and 1972 with miniature cups. The year 1919 was the first appearance of the three-handled loving cup we all know so well, and 1972 was the last year before it became part of the ceremony to present miniature cups to the winning trainers and jockeys. So, when we got to Bart, we needed to present to him the 1965, 1966 and 1967 Melbourne Cups. It had been Valmae who pushed the VRC to start presenting the miniatures from 1973, so Bart was most supportive of the initiative. I informed Bart we would be presenting the trophies to him and that, in fact, he would also be receiving an additional trophy for his

father, Jim Cummings, who had trained Comic Court in 1950. Naturally, Bart was thrilled.

On the day, Bart was juggling four miniature Melbourne Cup trophies. As we were standing there in the mounting yard at Flemington, with Bart's hands obviously full, I mentioned to him that, as of 2005, the VRC committee would also be presenting the breeder of the Cup winner with a miniature. Holding the trophies and looking me squarely in the eye, he said cheekily, 'I bred one of them too!'. Of course he was referring to 1996 winner Saintly. Knowing the VRC was not going to present the breeders' cups retrospectively I looked at him holding all those cups and said, 'I think you have enough, Bart.' He just flashed that familiar, cheeky smile that said so much more than any words. He went on to train Viewed, the 2008 winner, adding to his collection.

To most of the racing world, Bart was and will always remain the master of the wit-drenched one-liner, but there were times when he could truly open up and become deadly serious. For me, this would happen on those few private occasions—usually during the drive to or from the airport or while killing time prior to PR engagements. On this one occasion we started talking about a few random things before getting to the topic of artificial tracks and training surfaces. I don't think he drew breath for 20 minutes! He held to the firm view that a galloping horse places its hoof squarely and with massive force on the ground, creating a series of shockwaves that move rapidly and powerfully through the skeletal structure. That shock, said Bart, must dissipate somewhere. With artificial surfaces, he was adamant that the force incurred while galloping moved *up the leg of the horse as opposed to out of the leg*, as he believed the case when a galloper is on turf. He was adamant that artificial surfaces can do damage to horses. His assessment of training tracks was extensive, and while I don't profess to know anywhere near what he did, it was hard to question his logic. Bart obviously understood the horse and the forces placed on them at an early age.

On another occasion he talked about how he tried to lobby the VRC committee back in the 1970s to build a special, 2500-metre course at Flemington to cater for the classic Derby distance. He thought the run to the turn out of the straight from the 2500-metre gates came too soon for a full field of 3YOs to negotiate. His vision was to position the start in the centre of the course and angled towards Chicquita Lodge, on the Kensington side, and thus provide a sweeping turn as horses came out of the new, long chute towards the Maribyrnong River for the first time. He had a captive audience—but not the industry funds required to support his vision.

I am sure, as well, that Bart had a photographic memory. A few years back, when he stood waiting to be interviewed in Federation Square the day before the Cup was to be run, a random punter leaned over the fence and asked him for an autograph. He was happy to oblige, as always, but surprised to be handed the 1967 Melbourne Cup raceday book. This was the year the Cummings-trained Red Handed, ridden by Roy Higgins, outstayed Red Crest. He stood stock still, flicking through the pages and recalling the runners as if it had all taken place the day before. He went through each of the Cup starters, pointed out the key chances and discussed the quality of the different sires

> "
> Bart tried to lobby the VRC to build a special, 2500-metre course at Flemington to cater for the classic Derby distance.
> "

at the time. His recall was phenomenal. From all accounts this gift stood him in great stead when he was selecting yearlings. He could recall the many progeny of equine lines he had trained over the decades and what traits were consistent throughout the generations. He picked up many a champion performer based on that amazing memory and, of course, his remarkable intelligence and years of experience.

Bart was the complete package. He was a very good communicator, a talent underpinned by his emotional intelligence. He had a great appreciation of the horse, was a perpetual student of pedigrees and form, and he was equally comfortable talking big numbers with people of affluence. Like so many of his horses he had the right temperament: he was, above all, patient. What was it that he said so often? "Patience is the cheapest thing in racing and it is so seldom used." With a national propensity

to promote early 2YO races, you would have to agree. No wonder we can't get a look in these days when Europeans come to Melbourne at Cup time.

I often have also wondered if, had Bart not struck financial trouble in the late 1980s, would we still be reflecting on 12 Melbourne Cup victories? I am sure he would rather not have endured such stress at the time, but there is every evidence, at least as far as I am concerned, to suggest that this period of adversity was when he really became focused. Champions never lie down and he was just that—a champion. As his son, Anthony, said so succinctly in his eulogy at Bart's funeral, 'There hasn't been a bridle made that could hold him back.'

Four Cup wins in the 1990s are proof enough to suggest that Bart's mojo was stronger than ever during the latter part of his career, with the wonderful So You Think, winner of the 2009

and 2010 Cox Plates, the cream on Bart's cake as he moved into his silver-haired eighties.

What a record: an amazing 12 Melbourne Cups; seven Caulfield Cups; five Cox Plates; four Golden Slippers—and plenty more in between.

Farewell, Bart, you were unique. And your legacy will not be just that extra shine you put on the Melbourne Cup, it will be the immense good you did the entire racing industry.

Surely, you were A+.

JOE MCGRATH has been the manager of the Emirates Melbourne Cup Tour since its inception in 2003. He has worked, in two separate stints, for the VRC since 1987; been a raceday judge on Victorian racetracks, director of the Australian Racing Museum and Australian Racing Hall of Fame, and was once the editor of the Victorian Racing Calendar, later renamed Inside Racing. His mother, Kath, owned the great mare Bellition, who led 100 metres from the post before finishing seventh to Red Handed in the 1967 Melbourne Cup.

MIKED UP:
A regular at VRC functions and luncheons, Bart usually held the audience in the palm of his hand, unless it was holding one of the dozen Melbourne Cups he claimed.
PHOTO VRC COLLECTION

The man who would be king

Learning from a master trainer, caring for a champion racehorse before our greatest race and dreaming of even bigger things to come. **SHANE MCNALLY** describes how these factors helped mould a young Bart Cummings into one of the greatest thoroughbred trainers the world has seen.

H e grew up during World War II in Glenelg, that seaside refuge from the baking heat and searing desert winds that so often make Adelaide summers exercises in sweaty torment and endurance. Cool water and colder beer, the suburb was and remains a playground to most, but not for the teenager destined to become one of the greatest trainers the world has seen. The game was in his blood. Bart's father, Jim, had learned his horse sense breaking brumbies in Alice Springs, skills and insights that paid their greatest dividend in 1950, when the remarkable and versatile Comic Court brought home the Melbourne Cup.

As Bart later explained, there was never any doubt he would follow in his father's footsteps, even allowing for ironic allergies to horses and hay. "I couldn't be a jockey and I wasn't educated for anything else," he would explain many years later, "so that was what I did." Indeed, even medical advice couldn't sway his determination to make good. Straight after being told by his doctor that staying away from stables would cure his sniffles, he was back at work for his dad, learning his trade by "watching, listening and keeping my mouth shut".

Bart was 22 and working as a strapper for his father when he led the brilliant weight-for-ager Comic Court around the Flemington mounting yard minutes before the world's best, richest and most prestigious two-mile race got under way. Comic Court wasn't supposed to win; he was a champion middle-distance galloper who had won a string of races as a two-year-old, the Victoria Derby and St Leger the following year, and then added the Memsie, Craiglee, Turnbull, Mackinnon and Alister Clark to his honour roll at four. As a five-year-old, he kept winning weight-for-age races. After his mount failed in the Caulfield Cup, jockey Jack Purtell jumped off to give Pat Glennon the ride on that first Tuesday in November.

Despite bouncing back with his second Mackinnon, he was a highly-weighted performer in what punters thought was the wrong race, expected to fade from the top of the straight. Somehow, Jim Cummings trained him to carry the 59.5kg, cover the two miles and, incredibly, dominate the field from the clock tower and leave the likes of Chicquita, Morse Code and Alister to eat his dust as he bolted home in record time. A year later, Bart would deliver the great stallion across the border to start his stud career at Victoria's Warlaby Stud at Oaklands Junction, 23km north of Melbourne. Writing in *The Argus*, Tom Moon noted:

"He (Cummings) was obviously upset as he handed over the stallion. 'I don't suppose I'll ever have the chance to look after another one like him.' he said dejectedly." Little did he know! Comic Court would be no great success at stud, although he did sire Bart's first Cup runner, Asian Court, who finished 12th to Baystone in 1958.

During these early years Bart did as he said: he watched and learned. Comic Court's unexpected Cup victory was a pivotal moment for a young man determined to be a horse trainer. Years later, Bart would perform a similar trick. After training

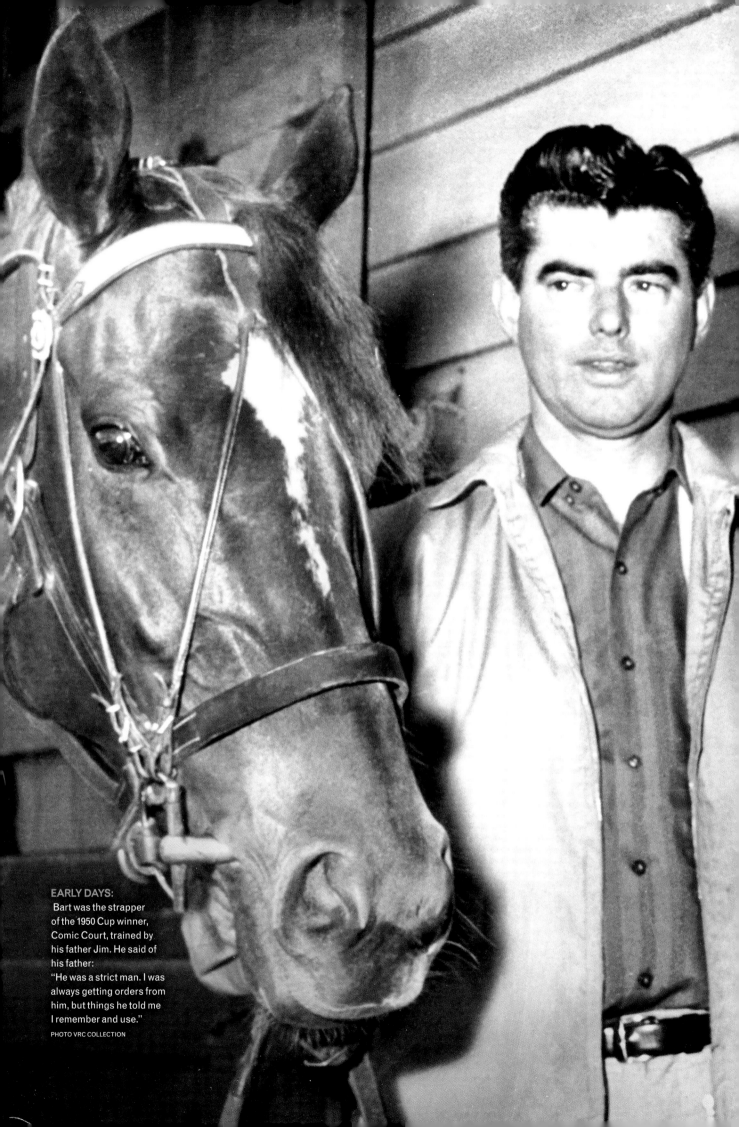

EARLY DAYS:
Bart was the strapper of the 1950 Cup winner, Comic Court, trained by his father Jim. He said of his father:
"He was a strict man. I was always getting orders from him, but things he told me I remember and use."

PHOTO VRC COLLECTION

lowly rated Think Big to perform on the day and over the two-mile trip, he watched the bay gelding beat a field of champions that included Leilani, Battle Heights and Igloo. The following year, just to prove that it had been no fluke, Think Big repeated the effort. Like his father, Bart had the knack of getting his runners right for the day, for the moment.

Think Big's victories would be more than 20 years in the future when Bart, then 22, led Comic Count around Flemington's mounting yard. Just three years after that 1950 Melbourne Cup, Bart became caretaker of the Glenelg stable when his father and mum, Nancy, took an overdue holiday to Ireland. The trip lasted months longer than expected and the South Australian stewards would have none of a foreman looking after a prominent stable for such an extended period. They insisted Bart apply for his trainer's licence. It was the end of his days working for anyone else. Bart would be his own man from that point on, but it wasn't an easy push to win his place among the training greats. Now out on his own after holding his father's stable together during his absence, the young Cummings had few horses in his barn, and it took almost two years to land the first winner under his shingle when Wells saluted at Morphettville. Then, slowly at first, the tally of his winners began to grow. Success breeds success and he began to see better horses placed in his care. By 1958, when Stormy Passage claimed the South Australian Derby, Bart inscribed the first entry in what would be a lustrous ledger of 268 Group 1 winners (as they were to be later graded).

A young star had arrived on the Adelaide racing scene but there was a lot of work to do before Bart would become a serious player on the national stage. He would also need to overcome some serious setbacks. Melbourne Cup victories looked a million miles away when the stewards opened an investigation into the winning performance of Cilldara at Morphettville in 1961 following a major form reversal after blinkers had been applied. At his previous start, Cilldara had finished last in a maiden over 1000m at Gawler. The use of blinkers had only recently been allowed in South Australia. The charge was upheld and the 33-year-old was banned from training for 12 months. Cummings appealed without success, but his sentence was later reduced by a month for his previous unblemished record.

It was a massive interruption for a man who was just making his mark. His first Melbourne Cup runner, Asian Court, failed in 1958, but the following year he landed the Underwood–Mackinnon double with high-class galloper Trellios, which went on to finish sixth in the Cup. By the autumn of 1963, though, things were looking up when he prepared The Dip, older

brother to the famed Light Fingers, and watched it win the Chipping Norton (then 2100m) at Randwick. A few months later, Anna Rose gave him his fifth Group 1 in the Thousand Guineas at Caulfield, and he claimed his second SA Derby in 1964 with the outstanding Ziema. In the spring of that year, he took the Wakeful and VRC Oaks double with Light Fingers, who went on to win the AJC Oaks the following autumn.

Later that year, the foundations of a legend were laid when Light Fingers wore down Ziema to win by the narrowest margin and give Bart not just his first Melbourne Cup but the quinella, the first of five similar finishes in the big race. Amazingly, the only times he trained the second placegetter in the

Cup, it was when he had trained the winner. The Light Fingers-Ziema finish was a remarkable result, made easier perhaps by a spectacular three-horse crash as the field passed Chicquita Lodge. The horses cleared out to have the stage to themselves over the final furlong, leaving champions, including a young Tobin Bronze, in their wake. "It was the first time I'd had great success," he said at the time, "and it left an indelible impression on my mind. I felt on top of the world." The win reinforced his belief in the power of positive thinking: "If you aim to do something, you'll achieve it."

And achieve he did. He had watched and learned well from his father, not least how to train a stayer. But he was much more than that. Months later, he would add further lustre to his list of notable successes when the brilliant Storm Queen (Anna Rose's sister) collected the 1996 Golden Slipper, a victory that was the high point in a string of wins. And through it all, over the course of those many and often improbable triumphs with sprinters, milers, fillies, colts and juveniles the sometimes awkward, always endearing humility of the man who gathered a dozen Cups on his mantelpiece never changed.

SHANE MCNALLY is one of Australia's most experienced racing journalists. Based in Adelaide, he has been a contributor to The Thoroughbred Times in the US, the British Racing Review and Australia's Racetrack magazine.

TASTE OF THE CUP:
It was 1950, and the brilliant Comic Court had led the Cup field a merry dance to claim victory for trainer Jim Cummings and jockey Pat Glennon. That's Bart on the right of the photo, striding to the stalls to prepare for the return of the champions.

The secrets of the Cups King

Like so many others who have tried to grasp the essence of Bart Cummings' reign atop the Australian turf, **STEPHEN HOWELL** can't quite put a finger on his secrets. But those who worked with him and were influenced by him have provided their special insights.

Millions of words have been written about Bart Cummings, and scores of writers have tried to get to the essence of the man, attempting to define his legend. (Phar Lap in 2007 and Cummings in 2008 were named Legends in racing's Hall of Fame, the first to be raised from their 2001 inaugural member status to Legend.)

No writer has got it 100 per cent right; almost certainly none ever will. *The Sydney Morning Herald* racing writer Max Presnell summed it up best when he told of a conversation he once had with Cummings' faithful Flemington work rider Joe Agresta, who said: "If you think you know Bart, you don't know Bart." In his outstanding farewell to Bart in the *Herald Sun,* after Bart's death, Les Carlyon who got to know him better than any other writer, described him as "unknowable".

And Bart never made it easy for those outside his exclusive stable. He never courted the media in the style of his great peers of the 1960s-1980s, Tommy Smith and Colin Hayes, and their children and successors Gai Waterhouse (née Smith) and David Hayes. One thing most who have written about Cummings agree on is that he was a shy man, preferring the company of a precious few to many, and preferring even more the company of horses.

His shield was a collection of one-liners, used increasingly as his achievements climbed from already extraordinary peaks in what has become the "open" era of racing. The simple answer, when cameras and microphones are thrust under your nose, is

THEN THERE WERE NINE: A hearty laugh to enjoy the moment, in October 1996 to promote the Cup. By then there were nine Cups in the Cummings' trophy cabinet. A month later Saintly made it 10, then came Rogan Josh (1999), and Viewed (2008).

to deflect. Mirrored aviator sunglasses, which he often wore, and very few well-chosen words did this best, deflecting, diverting, avoiding.

Cummings, until the end, remained old school. His business was his business, and the less he said the less he gave away. Agresta provides another example. The loyal servant, when he finished talking with Cummings at trackwork at Flemington walked across to talk with me for an interview in *The Age* a few days before the 2006 Cup—one his boss *didn't* win; Japan's Delta Blues did. At the end of the interview Agresta said that Bart's parting words to him were, "Don't forget, loose lips sink ships". Agresta added that the boss often said, "Keep your eyes and ears open and your mouth shut".

That never changed. Nor did Bart, in that sense. However, as his legend grew either side of his 12th Cup, he was being wheeled out more and more as the face of racing. And what a recognisable face: for achievements and for profile (both senses); for eyebrows; and, above them, for coiffure.

But Media Street was never a comfortable fit for such a shy man, no matter how much experience he had. He was much more at home in the stable and on the training track. This was where his genius expressed itself. Why so successful? Simply, he put horses first. He was patient with them, fed them well and trained them to be comfortable in their races; to finish off, and to finish off the opposition. On the eve of

the 2006 Cup, Cummings provided some insights to Danny Power, in an interview published in the VRC racebook on Cup Day. He began with his philosophy in a sentence: "The cheapest thing in racing is patience, and it's the most seldom used, so I do it the cheap way—plenty of time and patience. That's paid off for me handsomely." He was, of course, downplaying the unidentifiable, unknowable characteristics that make up genius: he had the instinct, the eye, the knowledge. He knew when to be patient, and when to push the envelope.

He also knew that the fundamentals rarely changed, particularly when it came to training stayers: "It remains the same. You need a horse with a staying pedigree, that has a good turn of foot, a good constitution and a trainer capable of teaching a horse to relax." In other words if the basics are there, the master trainer will do the rest.

Sports columnist Patrick Smith wrote in *The Australian* after 2008 Melbourne Cup winner Viewed won the 2009 Caulfield Cup, "The very word (Cummings) describes a mastery, a level of excellence that is difficult to comprehend and impossible to mimic. He has perfected horse training."

Cummings said as much in his ghosted *Bart: My life,* published during the 2009 Spring Carnival (*Bart: My life, by J.B Cummings, Macmillian, 2009*): "You really have to love the horse and read its moods. A lot of trainers don't put themselves inside the horse's skin, and don't ask themselves why horses are behaving a certain way. Horses are always sending you messages, and you need to learn their language ... You need to have empathy."

The Melbourne Cup, the highest of Cummings' many peaks, is a long time in climbing. Take Galilee, his 1966 winner and, as he says in *Bart: My life,* "he might have been the best staying horse I ever trained".

Cummings, in 2009, told a devoted audience at Tuesdays at Champions, a series of interviews at the Australian Racing Museum in Melbourne, that he bought Galilee cheaply as a yearling, for 3200 guineas, because the young horse's front legs were turned in. "Tommy Smith told me, 'Bart, you bought a bloody cripple'," Cummings said, mimicking Smith's squeaky voice. "After it won the Sydney Cup, I said, 'That bloody cripple's going all right, Tommy'." Galilee had carried 9st 7lb (60.5kg) to win the Sydney two-miler in the autumn after his Melbourne Cup win with 8st 13lb (56.7kg).

Cummings' other favourite was Saintly, his 1996 Cup winner. "Saintly was something special, I thought," he said that night at Champions, and offered a favourites order of sorts: Saintly and other Cup winners Galilee and Light Fingers, and the miler Shaftesbury Avenue.

Ten years after Saintly won Bart his 10th Cup, Cummings was like a proud father as he pointed out the horse at Flemington. "There's Saintly there, the old chestnut, Saintly 14-year-old," he said of the regular visitor for the Cup parade through the city (and to what Cummings called the 'old folks home', Living Legends at Greenvale on Melbourne's northern fringe) after making the trip from Princes Farm on the Nepean at the foot of the Blue Mountains, Cummings' property near Sydney, where the gelding is gainfully and happily employed in a nanny role. At the same time Cummings corrected me for calling the Melbourne stables Saintly Lodge with a simple, "Saintly Place".

At the time, Saintly was doing light trackwork, trotting and cantering. Agresta recalled that race jockey Darren Beadman rode him in trackwork over 2000 metres on the Saturday morning before the Cup win: "We were up in the stand and Bart kept looking at his (stop) watch. I didn't have a watch, but I thought, 'Oh geez, that's pretty good.' And Bart said, 'Don't tell anybody'."

From one of the trainers' towers in the middle of Flemington 10 years on, Bart said: "Everyone loved this horse. He was Australia's favourite. Mine, too." Saintly was the only one of Cummings' dozen Cup winners that he bred himself.

Bart said at Champions of his 11 winners of 12 Cups, "Different horses, different colours, different prices, different owners," but he added that key to winning was in the trainer's eye. "What your eye tells you is the way you should go," was his attitude in preparing each. For example, Light Fingers, who beat stablemate Ziema by a lip in 1965, did not need the same hard work as the runner-up. "The other horse was thoroughly fit," he said. "She was a bit better. My brother (Pat Cummings, a big punter) put a lot of money on Ziema."

Bart occasionally admits to having backed one himself, but never with any detail. More than likely the comment is another one-liner. After Sirmione won the Group 1 Mackinnon Stakes (2000m) at odds of $61 at Flemington on Derby day in 2007, Cummings, grin forming, said it was nice to come out ahead with both a winning bet and the prizemoney. But "it's the sport that counts, really," he continued. "You know that, don't you?" Sure, Bart.

Money rules in racing, a business as much as a sport, and for a time from the late 1980s Cummings had money problems. He calls the chapter in *Bart: My life* referring to the period "Betrayed" and he explains that, advised by big accounting firms, he spent $22 million in 1989 on yearlings in a bullish market for what had been named the Cups King Syndicate. Recession and rising interest rates meant he could not get people to buy into the syndicate. He believed losses would be shared with his accountant backers, but found that he carried the can alone.

A fire sale of 64 yearlings at Newmarket in Sydney netted a mere $9 million and Cummings faced a debt of $11 million to bloodstock agents, a sum compounded by legal fees when the Federal Court rejected his claim against the accounting firms. He sold assets, was able to negotiate an arrangement to pay 75 per cent of his income to creditors, and kept training winners. Among them were his ninth and tenth Melbourne Cup winners, Kingston Rule (1990) and Let's Elope (1991).

Such a setback would have destroyed lesser men; Cummings, then in his early 60s, remained true to his philosophy of looking ahead, never back, and prospered all over again. Among his biggest supporters was Malaysian property tycoon Dato Tan Chin Nam, who had part-owned the dual Cup winner Think Big (1974, '75) and was to own two more trained by Cummings, Saintly and Viewed, as well as Cummings' last great champion, So You Think. Tan Chin Nam's colours (black and white checks, yellow sleeves, black and white checked cap) have come to be just as recognised as Cummings' own, the proudly Australian green and gold diagonal stripes and white cap. In 2013, acknowledging Cummings' 60th year as a trainer, and his contribution to the racing industry, the Australian Racing Board and

"Cummings, then in his early 60s, remained true to his philosophy of looking ahead, never back, and prospered all over again."

Racing NSW paid tribute by preserving these famous colours for at least the next 50 years, preserved for the Cummings' family.

He owed much to the loyalty of Chin Nam, but even more to the man who helped him understand horses, Jim Cummings. But even praise for his father was played down. At Champions, Cummings described his mentor as a patient and dedicated man who said his prayers every night and "didn't put up with fools". The way Bart tells it, his parents going on a long holiday to Ireland forced his hand in taking out his licence because South Australian racing officials insisted he was doing more than merely minding the shop while his parents were away. "I was forced into the position I am in now, which is terrible," he said to much laughter.

The man who started out at Morphettville made his home ground at Randwick, with a Flemington satellite where he held court during big Melbourne meetings. Success followed a patient and largely prosperous path. The budding trainer who began in his father's shadow overshadowed him.

Those who knew Bart—or parts of him—or worked with him tend to explain his greatness with a direct simplicity: What they say is that Cummings thought of—and like—the individual horses in his care. That insight is perhaps best illustrated by the story Cummings told in his autobiography about Ming Dynasty, the grey who was unplaced in the 1977 and 1980 Melbourne Cups, the same years he won the Caulfield Cup. On retirement, Ming Dynasty was given to the Australian Jockey Club at Randwick as a clerk of the course's horse. Then, two years later and out of the blue, the old gelding turned up, on his own, at Leilani Lodge and went straight to his old box. As Bart said, "He appreciated a good home."

In the following interviews conducted in 2010, those involved with the great trainer—his son, his grandson, his jockeys, his foremen, his friends—told **ADRIAN DUNN** what makes the 'Cups King' tick.

ANTHONY CUMMINGS
Bart's son and Group 1-winning Randwick trainer

"My earliest recollections of Cup day are probably at school when everything would stop and the Melbourne Cup was broadcast across the school, which went through the PA system. Light Fingers (1965) is the first one I can remember. It was pretty exciting to sit in the classroom and have

all that happen around you. It was a great thing. I can remember going to trackwork with Dad in the pitch dark, freezing cold at Morphettville in the middle of winter, trying to find horses in the dark and clock them.

"My first Cup day at Flemington when Dad won was with Gold And Black (1977). That was exciting in itself, meeting the Governor-General (Sir John Kerr), ruddy faced and all. It was an exciting day. I've been there for most of them thereafter and had a small hand in a couple.

"I can also remember being in New Zealand and shown the rights and wrongs of yearlings, how to find the best ones. I think every foreman we had chased me out of the stables, obviously for good reason. I really enjoyed my time there, watching and learning and trying to make some sense of it. The basic tenets of what I've learned stem from what I learned at Dad's place. Learning about horses, as even Dad will tell you, is a never-ending story.

SON OF A GUN: Anthony Cummings has become a first-rate trainer in his own right, and has done his bit in continuing the Cummings line; his son James joined Bart in 2013 to form the Bart and James Cummings training establishment, and his other son Edward is Anthony's foreman.
PHOTO SLATTERY MEDIA GROUP

SOLDIERS IN ARMS

A photo for the ages, three great trainers together at Flemington after Bart Cummings (centre) had won his 12th Melbourne Cup, with Viewed. On the right is the affable Irishman Dermot Weld, whose mare Profound Beauty had finished a creditable fifth. Cummings "owns" the history of the Cup, but not far behind him is Weld, who pioneered the overseas interest in the Cup when he won with Vintage Crop (1993) and Media Puzzle (2002). It could be said that Vintage Crop's win changed the great race forever.

Cummings once described Weld as a "sweet-talking nice chap, who must have taken the handicapper out to dinner." Weld, who shared with the Cummings of latter years a reluctance to say much, did say of Cummings after the 2008 Cup: "He's simply amazing."

On the left is English-based Italian-born Luca Cumani, who had no reason to be smiling after his horse Bauer had failed to beat Viewed by a lip. The photo showed that Corey Brown, Bauer's rider, was ahead of Blake Shinn on Viewed, but it's that lip that counts! Cumani has vowed that to win the Cup is one of his great wishes.

After Cummings' death, Cumani offered his thoughts on the great man for this magazine. "Bart for many years has been Australian racing. Whenever anyone thinks of racing in that country they think of Bart Cummings. He's been a grandee of the training fraternity and was well respected throughout the world. The simple fact that he is being given a state funeral underlines the tremendous respect and admiration for him in Australia.

"I met him every time I went to Australia with one of my runners and he was always ready to dish out a one-liner about the Poms. On more than one occasion I had to remind him that I am a Wop and not a Pom. All in all, he was a great man and an exceptional trainer."

When Harry White pushed home Hyperno to win the 1979 Cup, he joined Bobbie Lewis as the only jockey to win the Cup four times. Three of White's wins were on Cummings' trained gallopers: Think Big (1974-5) and Hyperno (1979). His fourth, Arwon (1978) was for that other great trainer of stayers, George Hanlon.

"Where do you start with understanding Bart? Having an idea in your head of what you want to achieve, having the confidence to follow it through ... confidence, preparedness to persevere, doggedness. There are plenty of hurdles that can jump up and distract you if you're built that way. My old man isn't. He just gets on with the job and that's come through in quite a few different ways over the years. Plainly, he has a great eye for a horse and is one of the best trainers Australia has ever seen.

"Funnily enough, he says the best trainer he's ever seen is his father. I didn't get to see my grandfather that much, but the best trainer I've seen is my father. Hopefully, that gets to continue on. What sets him apart? Just following things through. He has an absolute determination to get the result, to the extent that such an attribute is unusual in anyone, let alone horse trainers.

"What he's done is pretty amazing. When you consider it (the Melbourne Cup) was a closed shop and now it is the race of the world and yet he continues to beat all and sundry. He has a view about the race and what is required and he's continually proven correct. Despite all the various themes and variations, he just goes along, pretty much sticks to a routine and, given the vagaries of horses, there's slight modifications. But at the end of the day he has a routine that plainly works. Horses are given the time they need to be what they can be. There was never any question about doing it any other way and that's a hard thing to learn.

"Does one Cup winner stand out? Viewed's win (in 2008) was sensational as much because he took on horses from the world stage. Saintly (1996) was pretty exciting. The Cox Plate has come to the fore as a world-class race and while he has always worked his campaign around the Caulfield Cup and from there into the Melbourne Cup, Saintly having come from Sydney gave him an opportunity to do it a little differently and still get the main prize. People doubted Saintly could stay, but again he showed the benefit of Dad's training style and what it allows horses to do.

"There's a huge sense of pride in what he's achieved, he's inspired me to follow my career and shaped a lot of who and what I am."

HARRY WHITE
Cup winner on Think Big (1974-75) and Hyperno (1979) for Cummings

"I've got no doubt Bart would have been successful in any walk of life. That's just Bart; he has that business brain.

"He was very good to ride for because he let the jockey relax. When someone told him I had a nap before Think Big won his second Cup, Bart said to the press, 'That's good. I like a relaxed jockey going into a big race.' That didn't worry him, he thought it was terrific. He didn't like having a nervous jockey on his horse. And he preferred you winning without the horse having to be flogged.

"Bart wouldn't anchor you with instructions. He would say to me, 'Have you a plan?' I'd say, 'Yeah, I've got a plan,' and he'd say, 'It's better having a plan than no plan.'

"The only time he gave me instructions in a Melbourne Cup was the second year Think Big won. He said you can't do what you did last year because he has so much more weight. He said ride it patiently and look for the shortest way home. I did what he said. It was a bog track and I never left the fence.

"It's hard to know if Bart was happy after the Cups I won with Think Big (at 12/1 and 33/1) because the second horse (which he trained— Leilani, 7/2 favourite, 1974; Holiday Waggon, 7/1, '75) was more fancied.

"Bart would always spend a lot of time watching the horse before and after they were worked and he loved walking his horses. It's one of the best things for a horse.

"He'd never say, 'This is a certainty', but he'd love you telling him it was. I remember trialling Cap d'Antibes down the straight before the (1975) Newmarket. It trialled beautifully and Bart said, 'What do you think?' and I said, 'All I know is that it's a champion.' Cap d'Antibes won the Newmarket and Bart said after I came back, 'You were right.'

"There was a time (1978) when we had a falling out. He got (foreman) Leon Corstens to tell me my services were no longer required, so I thought, 'Things are going no good here,' so I went to England. I came back and won the Cup on George Hanlon's horse, Arwon. I remember I won a race for Colin Hayes on the day Arwon won the Cup and Bart's horse ran second. He lent over from the second stall and said, 'I've done you a favour.' That was Bart's way of saying sorry. It was as good as an apology as you could get from Bart.

"Bart is a one-off. He doesn't worry about things. I reckon the roof could fall in and Bart wouldn't worry. He doesn't show any emotion, but deep down I think he's a sensitive person."

JOHN MARSHALL
Cup winner on Rogan Josh (1999)

"I was due to ride Ruy Lopez for Bart in the Cup, but he had to run one-two in the Geelong Cup to qualify. Damien Oliver rode him, box-seated him and through no fault of his couldn't get a run in the straight (and finished ninth). I got to the track (at Randwick) the next day pretty dejected that I'd missed out on my Cup ride. Bart noticed I was down. He said, 'Don't worry, I've got another ride for you.' He said I could go to Melbourne on Saturday and ride it in the Mackinnon. I thought, 'Here we go, a hack ride in the Cup, just making up the numbers.' That's all he said. It could have been Phar Lap or a donkey, he never really elaborated on those things. He was always very dry.

"It turned out to be Rogan Josh. He wins the Mackinnon and then wins the Melbourne Cup. In my seven previous Cup rides, I'd had a couple

CURRYING FAVOUR: John Marshall rode Bart's 11th Cup winner, the aptly named Rogan Josh, a son of Old Spice. Marshall said later: "Anyone who has ridden for Bart will tell you that every horse will be cherry ripe for his target race." Rogan Josh won the Mackinnon Stakes-Cup double in brilliant style, and Marshall would be a Cup ambassador for many years.

of half-chances, but never a real solid chance. I went into the Cup thinking this is a realistic chance to win the Cup. I'd been riding for Bart on and off for 10 years. I knew whatever that horse did in the Mackinnon he was going to improve upon. Having ridden for Bart for so many years, I knew that Bart would have him cherry ripe on Melbourne Cup day. Anyone who has ridden for Bart will tell you that every horse will be cherry ripe for his target race.

"Bart is the complete package. He has an eye for a yearling, a 'learned education' for breeding, the history of breeding and the mastery of being able to train horses at the highest level. I've seen trainers who are really good trainers, but need someone else to buy yearlings for them. Bart specifically buys the horses with the breeding to suit his style. I don't think he's ever bought dud ones.

"Bart was brilliant to work for. He's a man of few words, but working with him you learn so much. He doesn't have to say a lot to learn from him. He's just a genius. Bart's famous line to me was, 'Ride it like a stayer'. It didn't matter if you were in a 1000-metre race or two-day bike race. That's how he bought them, that's how he trained them and that's how he wanted them ridden. It was pretty simple if you rode for Bart—you rode them like a stayer."

PETER MASON
A Melbourne friend and client
for more than 30 years

"Bart's success is due to the fact that he is an incredibly intelligent person and he's incredibly observant, too. I don't see there is any mystery to it. Bart hasn't changed, but he keeps in touch and up to date with what's happening. His principles are the same, he follows the same patterns with his training and it is a successful one.

"Bart is very consistent and relies on his own thoughts and judgements. He's very alert and very alert to everything. When people speak to Bart they've usually got some agenda, but Bart is aware of that right from the start. He can work things out quicker than a lot of people. People forget Bart is also successful as a business person—he's been involved with Ranvet (a maker of veterinary medication and supplements) for a long time.

"He weighs things up, he doesn't overreact or panic or anything like that. He just sums things up. I don't suppose I have seen anybody as observant as Bart, and that goes to everything and everyone. Intelligent, street smart and observant, that's Bart."

STEVEN KING
Cup winner on Let's Elope (1991)

"Never during all the time I rode for him did Bart give me any instructions on how to ride Let's Elope. Not once. I was quite amazed that given she was such a high-profile horse running in all these big races—including the Caulfield and Melbourne Cups—that Bart didn't tell me how to ride her and what to do on her. He was always very calm. He would just say, 'You know her, ride her the way that suits,' and that was basically it. She was basically a backmarker and because she was so big, she was not a horse that you would try to weave through the field.

"Bart was so easy going; there was never any pressure on me and, for a 21-year-old, I appreciated that and it gave me confidence each time I rode her. Sometimes you can be overloaded with instructions, but that wasn't Bart's style with Let's Elope. Bart never came in spruiking her. I heard on the grapevine that Bart had backed her in doubles, but he never let on. He never put any pressure on me and, for me, that's the most memorable thing about him.

"I've ridden some good horses for him since— Never Undercharge (to win the Group 1 Stradbroke Handicap, 1400m, in 1993), Dane Ripper (to win the Group 1 Australian Cup, 2000m, in 1998)— and he was just the same. I don't think he's ever changed. If you ever rode a bad race, Bart wouldn't say anything, he would just take you off the horse. Every ride I had on Let's Elope I treated as if it was my last, and there were a lot of big jockeys ringing Bart to get the ride.

"He is always just so laid back, so patient, and I think you'll find that he's used mainly patient jockeys. I remember him telling me the cheapest thing in racing is patience, and he's spot on."

DARREN BEADMAN
Cup winner on Kingston Rule (1990)
and Saintly (1996)

"My first recollection of Bart was when I was 15 and just starting an apprenticeship with Theo Green when our stables were on High Street, Kensington, and Bart's Leilani Lodge was next door. Bart's stables and horses just stood out; just the attention to detail. Where other horses had normal towels or hessian bags, Bart's horses had saddlecloths and they carried his signature colours—yellow, green and white. You could tell he took a lot of pride in his place, that he was very meticulous.

"I can't remember my first meeting with Bart, but I can recall my first ride for Bart in a Group 1 race—More Rain in the (1983) Doncaster Handicap

(she was 18th of 20). I was 17. It was a massive thrill.

"After I rode five winners on Silver Slipper day (in 1990), I got a call from a Sydney journo, Keith Robbins, who said I was in the running to ride Kingston Rule in the Cup. Bart gave me the nod and I rode the horse in the Dalgety (now the Lexus Stakes, on Victoria Derby day) and he just said, 'Ride him like a stayer.' He said the run would tune him right up for the Cup, but not to knock him about with the whip. After he ran a solid second, I thought he was going to be a real live chance. Bart was then, and is now, pretty flat-line when it comes to building a jockey's confidence about whether the horse is a good thing.

"One thing about Bart is that he doesn't set his jockeys too much of a task, he doesn't tie you down with too many instructions. You don't feel under pressure and I think that is one of the reasons why he has the results that he does. Whenever you walked out of the jockeys' room to ride for Bart, you just felt comfortable. You don't feel the anxiety or pressure of a big race

and that's one of my real enjoyments of riding for Bart and being around Bart. He's very laid back and relaxed. I can remember T.J. Smith would be at trackwork in the middle of the night working his horses and, when he would be walking off the track, Bart would be walking on to the track. They were totally different identities. You could feel the tension with T.J, the urgency of it all, but with Bart it was like, 'What will be, will be. If the horse is good enough it will win.'

"Bart is such a great visionary, right from when the horses are foals and yearlings. Most of his horses don't pull, they're relaxed just like Bart. Saintly is a classic example. He looked like one of these big 14-year-old kids trying to play first grade football. He was big and gangly and not quite there. Bart just kept on putting him in the right races—he just has a wonderful thing with timing. He could place a horse at the right spot at the right time and not put too much pressure on a horse. Actually, after his run in the Metropolitan (at Randwick a month before the Cup), I lost a

REVERING THE LORD OF THE CUP:
Bart and Darren Beadman formed a great partnership through the nineties, with the win of Saintly in the 1996 Cup their high point. The partnership also may be remembered for one of Bart's marvellous one-liners—when Beadman decided to give up riding to become a minister of the church, claiming that he had spoken to God and He wanted Beadman to quit riding to become an evangelist, Cummings said: "I think he should seek a second opinion."

little bit of faith in the horse. I just thought he would win the Metrop (he finished a close third), but then Bart brings him back in distance and produces him in a really hot Cox Plate. I thought he had a good chance, maybe run a nice third or fourth, but not a winning chance. For him to win Australia's greatest weight-for-age race just illustrates the genius of Bart.

"What really surprised me was the work Bart poured into Saintly after the Cox Plate. He gave him some really, really strong gallops. He just does things that are outside the square, he's not bound by any training manual. What I've seen him do with one horse, he'll do the total opposite with another horse. I said to Bart on the Saturday morning before the Cup, 'This horse has got better.' He just smiled. Going into the Cup, I just thought he was a good thing.

"When I came back (after two years out in the late 1990s training for the ministry), I rode a lot for Bart, got to know him really well. He took me out to his farm for lunch, I got to be part of Bart's world. It was a real privilege."

JOHNNY MILLER
Cup winner on Galilee (1966)

“Bart was just getting into full-blast mode when Galilee came along. I think he even then had made up his mind that the easiest race on the Australian calendar to win was the Melbourne Cup. And, he just went from there. He was very easy to ride for; he never ever gave you instructions. The only time he gave me instructions was in the Caulfield Cup when I rode Galilee and he said, 'They tell me you need to be up in the first four,' and I said to him, 'Hang on a minute, he's never been up there in his life.'

"I remember Kel Gillespie wrote in the Adelaide *Advertiser* that Galilee was to be ridden out the back in the Caulfield Cup like it was a track gallop. Bart didn't worry. He never filled your head with instructions. Even when I got beaten on Galilee in the Epsom (over a mile at Randwick in 1966), all he said to me was, 'Didn't you see Chantal?' I ran second, came from last. Maybe I should have gone a bit quicker, a bit earlier. (Chantal, 7/4 favourite, won by five lengths from Galilee, 14/1.)

"Patience has always been Bart's calling card and it was no different with Galilee. He thinks about what he's going to do and plans in advance. Bart knew Galilee was special and I knew Galilee was special. In the (Melbourne) Cup I just let him amble around, rode him like he was in a track gallop, let him weave his way through the field and from the top of the straight it was virtually all over. I was very confident. He was a pretty special horse; he'd

handle it against today's horses, no worries.

"Bart is just one of those out-and-out specials. I still speak to Bart frequently. We don't talk too much about the past, we mainly talk about what is going to happen tomorrow. That's Bart. He's always looking forward, not living in the past."

ROY HIGGINS
Cup winner on Light Fingers (1965) and Red Handed (1967). [Roy Higgins died in 2014.]

“Bart is just the most perfect horse trainer one would ever want to be associated with, and he's a horse psychologist as well. In my early days with him we used to stand there for half an hour after riding the horses work and we'd talk about little idiosyncracies: little things that I felt in the work; doing this, doing that. He loved for you to be able to pinpoint what you thought was the problem, and he'd go to work on that. He was an absolute genius at changing …

when a horse has got ability and is not producing, obviously there's a reason out there. He would go in search of that reason, he'd work on the horse mentally, physically, in every area.

"Bart was a great listener; still is. He would love to hear you trying to sort out some little thing that was wrong with a horse and he'd go to work on that. And boy, nine out of 10 times he could correct it.

"And some of those results … I used to say Bart's not only proven that he can tune a horse to peak on the first Tuesday in November, he has tuned them to peak at three o'clock on the first Tuesday in November. That's how fine he was with them. Even the difference between the Saturday's races to the Tuesday with the horse, you could just feel the difference coming out. It was an incredible feeling. I think some of the greatest experiences around an animal in my life were those Bart was associated with."

LEON CORSTENS

Former stable foreman in Melbourne, now a trainer

"Where do you start? He's *the* man, he's a Trainer with capital T. What else can I say?

"Bart's expertise just topped everything off. Being away from horses for a little while, you just see a bit more than you do if you are around them all the time. He waits for the horse to come to him, he doesn't make it come to him. I remember Think Big coming across from New Zealand—he looked like a little pony. Bart kept him in the box for 18 months. He just said, 'Don't worry, he'll grow.' Bart always had great confidence in the horse. Even with Saintly, he just took his time. Things unfolded and he went from strength to strength.

"He just has the uncanny knack of getting the horses ready at the right time, especially around Melbourne Cup time. He just sticks to the same

GREAT TEAM:
For decades the team of Bart Cummings and Roy Higgins was peerless, with Higgins the number one rider for Cummings at all major meetings. They won two Cups together, 1965 with Light Fingers and 1967 with Red Handed, and had dozens of Group 1 winners together. Higgins once said that 80 per cent of his Group wins were on Cummings-trained gallopers. They did have a tiff in 1980, breaking up the partnership four years before Higgins retired as increasing weight made it impossible for him to continue. Their friendship was restored, as Higgins pursued a career in the media and as a bloodstock buyer and seller.

method, the one that his father used. He doesn't do anything any different and, as he said, if he does that and it doesn't happen then he knows it's not his fault, it's the horse. No good saying he's lucky—you can't be lucky 12 times, can you?

"You talk about the Melbourne Cups. What about the Newmarkets, what about the Lightning Stakes, what about the Derbys, what about the Australian Cups? You can just rattle them off again and again. It just goes to show that he loves doing what he's doing. You have to be good when he has the passion that he has. He's still the man."

NIGEL BLACKISTON
Former stable foreman in Melbourne, now a trainer

"Bart just has a canny knack of picking the right horse, getting it to the races at the right time and he's proven now at 81 (Cummings turned 82 in November 2009) that he can still get the job done. Remarkable. He's patient, when he knows he has a good horse, he nurses it when it's appropriate then pushes forward when it's needed. I've worked for some talented people and things don't work out for them, but with Bart it always just seems to fall into place.

"His foresight with purchases, feeding them and medical care ... Bart is on top of the game the whole way. I can remember when Let's Elope arrived and she was just this big, plain chestnut thing, and what sticks in my mind is that she used to eat everything. I remember saying to Bart, 'She can eat,' and Bart replied, 'Well, keep feeding her son, keep feeding her.' She was fantastic. She

had a great constitution. All Bart's good horses were very similar—good constitution, they eat well and they were big, powerful horses. Saintly, Rogan Josh, Kingston Rule—they were all big, athletic type of horses.

"Bart didn't let things worry him. For the first four years I was there he kept on saying to Leon (Corstens, the foreman before Blackiston), 'What's that 'Pommy' lad's name?' He didn't harp on things, he would say what he needed to say and move on. That's why he's been so good. He doesn't let things get on top of him, he just keeps ticking over at a nice, even keel."

LEE FREEDMAN
Hall of Fame trainer with five Melbourne Cup wins

"What makes Bart tick? Please, can you help me solve the global financial crisis or solve the problems in the Middle East? It would be easier. I think he has an undying passion for racing, that's what makes him tick. The rest flows from that. He has his own clock that he works, too. Once you are that good, you never lose it. He has a world of knowledge, he has a great memory and he's just outstanding at what he does.

"Obviously, when I moved to Flemington (in the 1980s after training in Sydney) and having access to seeing how he did things was a big thing for me. It was very interesting to see how he went about things, but I had contact with Bart before I moved to Melbourne. He had horses for my father and we often pre-trained the horses for him and he had even been to our place at Yass a couple of times. When I was forming in my own mind what I was going to do, meeting someone like Bart was a huge thing.

"He never changed. His hair just got whiter and his wit sharper."

JOE AGRESTA

Cummings' long-serving Flemington track rider

"Gai Waterhouse said to me after Viewed won the Melbourne Cup, 'How does Bart do it?' I said, 'Gai, if every trainer in Australia was told to follow what Bart does every day right up to Melbourne Cup day, I would guarantee that 99.999% of trainers would not follow it through. The only one who would do it is Bart.' I've been with Bart 30 years and he sets a plan and he just doesn't change from it. If a horse misses a run for some reason, Bart will work the horse, if he's right, over the distance of the race they missed, on the Sunday morning.

"Where other trainers ease up or cuddle horses going into the Cup, Bart keeps the work right up to them. He said to me after Kingston Rule won the Melbourne Cup if the horse can't handle the work, they can't win this race. He has nerves of steel. What makes him so good is that he has a plan and he does it no matter what.

"I remember wondering for the first 10 years I was with Bart if we were ever going to win another Melbourne Cup. I said to Bart about two years before Kingston Rule won, 'We're not going real well' and Bart just said, 'Don't worry son, just keep at it. We'll get there.'

"On the Saturday morning before the (2008) Cup, Bart asks me how I think Viewed is going. I tell him I think we're behind the eight-ball because we had missed a run with him. He just said, 'We'll be right.' The horse copped a little check in the Mackinnon (on the Saturday), but I thought he was disappointing. As he was about to leave the track, Bart told me to ring the jumping jockey because he planned to jump Viewed on the Sunday. And on the Monday morning, Bart told me to work him over 1600m and come home my last 600m.

"After Viewed won the Cup my heart was pounding, I was still shaking sitting up in the Terrace about 90 minutes after the Cup. I said 'I can't believe that horse won, Bart,' and he said, 'Yeah, might be a bit better than we thought.' And, then (pointing to the Southern Star in the distance) he says, 'See that big wheel? It hasn't moved for five or six days. It was supposed to be going four days ago, something's wrong there.' I'm thinking, what the … And, you know, Bart was right about the wheel (being damaged).

"He never gets flustered. You go to the stables on Melbourne Cup morning and you are running around like a blue-arse fly and Bart will say, 'Hey, Joe, have they watered these roses this morning?' Me or Reg (Fleming, the Melbourne stable foreman) will say, 'We've got to go to the races,' and Bart coolly says, 'The races will still be there in five minutes, let's get these roses watered.'

"What I admire about Bart the most is that when he went through that trouble with the syndication (in the early 1990s) is that he never changed. I was speaking to Val (Cummings' wife) and said, 'I love him.' I told her I thought we were gone, we didn't train a winner for two years, and this and that. And, Val said to this very day he never mentioned it. He would walk in the door and say, 'G'day Val, what's for dinner?' I thought to myself, what man could hold something like that and not go home and whinge and cry? He's just an extraordinary man."

REG FLEMING

Stable foreman in Melbourne

"One morning while we were at trackwork, Bart turned to me and said, 'Horse training is simply common sense, but many people don't use it.' He's a quiet man who thinks before he says or does anything. He's a great thinker; he has a great memory. If a horse has a problem, he can remember a similar situation and recall how he handled it and he can always fix whatever the problem is. He's a very patient man, very relaxed and that goes a long way to explaining why he's so good.

"Saintly was a champion, an out-and-out champion. Bart always knew that Saintly was something special … he was only just starting to warm up (when injury ended his career). He was an immature horse. Bart knew he couldn't handle running in a Caulfield Cup so close to the (1996) Melbourne Cup after he ran in the Metropolitan. And that's why he took him to the Cox Plate. Just little things like that; knowing his horses so well is what Bart is all about.

"Rogan Josh came to us with not bad form, but he quickly cottoned on to Bart's work like a duck to water. The more we fed him the better he got and that's why he won the (1999) Cup. Bart was happy with how Viewed was going coming into the (2008) Cup. He missed a run and hadn't had a run for a month going into the Caulfield Cup, but Bart was happy, especially with his last half-furlong. He had no luck in the Mackinnon, but Bart was really happy with him. The only reservation was that missed run, but in hindsight it may have helped him.

"How did Bart react after the Melbourne Cup? Just like he normally does. He keeps his emotions to himself—he's a funny man to work out. I've

HELPING HAND:
The combination of Bart Cummings as trainer and Dato Tan Chin Nam is one of the most enduring and most successful in racing history. Together they were part of four Cup victories: Think Big (1974-5), Saintly (1996) and Viewed (2008), and many other Group 1 victories. This photo was taken after the presentation ceremony for the 2009 Crown Oaks won by Faint Perfume, Bart's ninth in the Classic. Their partnership reached a crescendo in 2009 and 2010 with the glorious So You Think.
PHOTO SLATTERY MEDIA GROUP

worked for him for 15 years and have loved every minute of it.

"How would I describe Bart? He's … well, he's just a genius."

DATO TAN CHIN NAM
Cummings' best-known owner who has four Cup wins (Think Big 1974, '75; Saintly 1996; Viewed 2008)

"Bart leads the life he loves and loves the life he leads. It is a simple life. It is horses. A dedicated doctor goes from clinic to the hospital to a private home and then back to the clinic again. Bart's routine is stable, horse, racetrack then back to the stable again. At 4.30 am he is out at the track. You can see his eyes narrowing like a hawk when he watches the horses run, his strong mobile features held in check by a low, straight forehead. Bart knows what he sees because he is seeing what he knows better than any other trainer on earth.

"He has to be one of the luckiest and smartest men ever to live. He would have been a physicist or a top executive had he chosen another field. Bart embodies the difference between desire for success and greed. He calls himself a gentleman trainer who tries to conserve his horses, and in this probably lies his greatness. He treats two-year-olds gingerly and prefers not to race them heavily until they are three. Bart seldom works horses at top speed. He saves their speed and power for the actual race rather than wasting it on the training track.

" 'Where do trainers go wrong?' Bart asked me rhetorically once. 'The cheapest thing in training is patience and it's always the last thing used'."

(Excerpts from Dato Tan Chin Nam's *Never Say I Assume*, mph publishing)

DUNCAN RAMAGE
Dato Tan Chin Nam's bloodstock manager

"The record books show that Bart's brave enough and prepared enough to do things with horses that other people are not. He has a system and, yes, he's tinkered with the detail within that system and certainly upgraded it in varying areas as it has become available. And, he worked very closely with (leading veterinarian) Dr Percy Sykes, who was a pioneer in working on pathology with horses. Bart embraced that type of technology. He's very keen to embrace technology.

"If you're going to eat, you want to eat the best and Bart has employed the same principle with his horses. The right form of vitamins, amino acids all those sorts of things are very heavily studied. A lot of that came from observations he made from his late father, Jim.

"Bart applies a hell of a lot of common sense to what he does. The basic principles of what goes on in his Melbourne and Sydney stables are the same. Horses going from one stable to the other? It happens seamlessly.

"One of my earliest involvements with Bart was the collapse of the Cups King syndicates. The moral strength of the man at that time was amazing and, so too, was the moral strength of his wife, Val. She has been a very strong influence behind the scenes, a pillar.

"I don't think Bart has changed too much. One of his greatest assets is that he is very intuitive about both animal and human reactions, body language and their mind. He observes greatly. Bart has always said it pays to listen and observe. He said, 'You know what you know, but you may not know what the other person knows.' Bart is no shrinking violet, he's happy to call a spade a spade. He has an absolutely outstanding memory, he can visualise a horse and what potential it may have. It's an intuitive gift.

"Many people can get a horse fit, but there is a difference in getting a horse fit and making that horse excel to win those top races. You only get so many opportunities to win big races and that's what Bart is all about: winning big races. Bart has extreme patience with horses and humans; it may run out quicker with people than it does with horses. He always says you must visualise what could happen rather than limit yourself to the bad that may happen.

"Several years ago Bart had three runners in the Melbourne Cup. Two of them raced on Derby day, one in the Mackinnon, the other the Lean Cuisine (now known as the Lexus Stakes). The other had raced the previous Saturday at Randwick in the Tatts Cup. At trackwork at Flemington on the Monday, he worked the three of them over a mile and a quarter (2000 metres). They only went evens and improved a bit, but still the Melbourne Cup was the next day. He was the only trainer who had a Cup runner to work horses. Some trainers were saying, 'The old boy has lost it, finally lost his marbles. He's galloping his horses on the Monday, two of them raced on Saturday.' The net result was: Rogan Josh won, Zazabelle deadheated for third and the other horse (Rebbor) ran last. It's a clear example of Bart believing in his own judgment.

"He has a system and the records, by and large, show it works."

JAMES CUMMINGS

Bart's grandson James joined Bart in August 2013 to create the Bart and James Cummings training partnership. The partnership produced 11 Stakes winners (two of them Group 1). The horses were transferred to James' name after Bart's death.

"Besides the obvious—that he's a genius and the best horse trainer in the modern era and possibly in our whole history—what strikes me is that whatever he does, he always does with confidence.

"He devotes a lot of his time and a lot of his energy to his horses, but if things don't go right, it's not the end of the world. The expression on his face when he won the AJC Derby (with Roman Emperor in 2009) was as offhand as it is if he loses a midweek (race) at Canterbury. If his horse in the Golden Slipper gets held up for a run and should have won, he shrugs his shoulders and moves on. That horse will probably come out and win the Sires' Produce, or Champagne Stakes. He just doesn't let it bother him. That's what held him through thick and thin through the years.

"He can be effusive at times, but he keeps things to himself. He keeps his raw emotion in check so that his professionalism really shines through.

"He's my grandfather and I respect him for what he's achieved. He's an icon for the fact that he's successful, good at his craft. What I take from what he's done is that invariably he's done the right thing and he's done it with confidence. It doesn't surprise me that he's won Melbourne Cups after he turned 80. He's unflappable, he just keeps on going."

BLAKE SHINN
Cup winner on Viewed (2008)

"I still call him Mr Cummings. I've always called him Mr Cummings since I began riding for him as a 17-year-old. He just nods his head and says, 'Yes, son.' It's a mark of a respect. He's a legend, he's the greatest racehorse trainer in our history.

"It means everything to have won a Melbourne Cup for Mr Cummings, it's a privilege and an honour. Just to ride for him in the Melbourne Cup was an honour. It definitely gave me confidence that I was riding a horse for Mr Cummings and it gave me greater confidence that he thought he was a genuine chance. He thought he could win—he told me the horse (Viewed) was as good as he could get him. When you hear someone like Mr Cummings say that before you go out to ride in a Melbourne Cup, it makes you feel pretty good.

"It was very straight-forward riding for him. He made it clear in the simplest of terms how he wanted the horse ridden and that was basically ride him where he's happy, but get clear running from the 600 metres. He knows exactly where the horses race and all their patterns and where the best part of the track is."

STEPHEN HOWELL'S reports in The Age and The Sunday Age on November 3 and 4, 2006, and November 4, 2007, and reports from the track and from Tuesdays at Champions

The Australian, Patrick Smith column, October 19, 2009

Bart: My life, by J.B. Cummings, Macmillan, 2009

ADRIAN DUNN'S interviews with those who know Cummings

Never Say I Assume, by Dato Tan Chin Nam, mph publishing

The one-name phenomenon

'Cummings' is the surname that appears in the record books, but punters, friends, owners and, indeed, even those with only a passing interest in the racing game needed to hear only 'Bart' to recognise a synonym for excellence, as **STEPHEN MORAN** recalls.

Bart was Bart. No surname, no introduction required.

He was, of course, the 'Cups King', but so much more than that. He did, after all, train 256 Group 1 winners aside from the Cups. He was the master of the Classics; the sultan of the Straight Six; the trainer of trainers and the favourite of fans.

He was a man of his, and also another, time. Contemporary in his thinking—he was adamant that he never looked back—and yet he remained kind of old-fashioned. Softly spoken, slow to anger, understated, not boastful rather than modest. He often wore a tie to trackwork, especially in the early days. He went to Mass on Sundays.

He was, perhaps, to the racing public something like your much loved but occasionally grumpy old grandpa, with a touch of the Dalai Lama thrown in, and all beneath those famous eyebrows—a wise, old owl. Wise he was and witty too. The repetition of his many one-liners rarely made them tiresome.

Always laid-back, but never a pushover, he didn't tolerate fools and he was hard at times, no doubt, on his son, Anthony, who would follow in his footsteps, just as Bart followed his father. But he mellowed with the passing years. "I don't think I had a blue with him over the last couple of years and, at one stage, he even told me that I'd come good—rare praise indeed," Anthony Cummings said frankly in his eulogy to his father.

Near life-long friend Malcolm Wuttke, at the funeral, was on a similar track, "Bart loved his children but sometimes found it hard to express that." The standard line from his son, over the years, has been that "Bart taught me everything I know, but not everything he knows." Less well known is that, in 2006, Bart said: "All I know about horses and training was what my father did … not that he ever explained anything to me."

Bart's attitudes were spawned in another time, another era. He was born in 1927, two years before the Great Depression, which says more about the span of his life than simply noting that he was all of 87 years old when he died. His father, Jim, was born in the tiny South Australian hamlet of Eurelia in 1885. His forebears, who in those days spelled their name 'Cummins', were among the most prominent settlers in a township that now barely exists.

Nothing could better encapsulate the demands of that other, distant time than Cummings' own memory of his father "joining his uncle at the Ellery Creek station, west of Alice Springs, where they'd round-up brumbies, shoe them, feed them and prepare them for sale to the Indian army. That business ended when motorised vehicles took over from the horses."

In an essay on Eurelia, *southaustralianhistory.com* devotes several paragraphs to the Cummin(g)s family and quaintly observes "the Cummings have been involved with horses and racing for a long time. Jim Cummings' son, Bart, has become a well-known trainer." I'm sure the man who came to be so well known by his Christian name alone, not to mention the 'Cups King' moniker

FANS FOREVER:
The sign says it all, and it speaks for all racing folk. No personality in racing has not only transcended the sport, but done it with unfailing integrity, and a warm relationship with the punting brigade; we all loved Bart whether backing him, or watching as his charge wore us down. This was one of those days when the whole crowd cheered as Faint Perfume ($1.65 favourite), ridden by Michael Rodd, won the VRC Oaks.
PHOTO SLATTERY MEDIA GROUP

RING A DING DING
IT'S ANOTHER
ONE FOR
THE KING

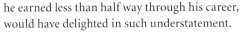

he earned less than half way through his career, would have delighted in such understatement.

Bart's most recent five or six Cup winners were probably superfluous to his reputation and a diversion from the truth of his unrivalled record in major races of all types over any distance. His first six Cups, of the 12 he took home, secured him the mantle as the Melbourne Cup's most successful trainer, and the title of 'Cups King'

Way back in November, 1974, journalist and turf aficionado Les Carlyon began an article on the great trainer by using just his forename. "Bart is the man everyone wants to know …" Carlyon began, "It is as improbable as racing itself that such a cult should exist around a man who says so little. Bart is, first of all, shy. He speaks sparingly, as though he is saving the best thoughts for himself, which he is."

At that time, Cummings had just trained Think Big to win the Cup—'just' his fourth success in the race. And yet, in that same article, Carlyon presumptuously, outrageously (or with great prescience and perspicacity) also wrote: "… he may be—there is no sensible way of proving these things—the finest racehorse trainer in the world."

So, 21 years into his training career (there would be another 40!), Cummings had certainly come of age in the eyes of the respected Carlyon, whose judgment, for better or for worse, was never clouded by the punt. Cummings had also, even then, won over the more hard-nosed—who argue that a racing opinion is only verified by a wager—by producing a raft of top class-horses right through the sprinting to staying spectrum. These were horses that sustained their performance over more than one season with multiple major race wins. These were runners who debunked the myth that Cummings' one and only specialty was preparing horses for the Cup and only the Cup, horses who rewarded punters and owners who maintained the faith. These included Storm Queen, a jittery and highly strung filly requiring a special brand of insight and empathy. "I didn't dare work her when she became excited," Cummings explained. He managed that skittish temperament to see her win, at two, the Merson Cooper Stakes (forerunner to the G1 Blue Diamond); what is now the G2 VRC Sires' Produce Stakes; the G1 Golden Slipper and the G1 Champagne Stakes. She was his first Group 1 winner short of 1600 metres.

Cummings was not at Rosehill to see Storm Queen win the Slipper. "I really had to think about it," he later recalled. "The Queen Mother was in Adelaide and had been asked to present the Birthday Cup trophy. I had Galilee running in the race and the SAJC (South Australian Jockey Club) asked me to be on hand for the presentations especially if I thought Galilee would win. 'Oh,

he'll win all right,' I told them so that was that. I heard the Slipper being broadcast over the course speakers during the presentation. The race caller said that Storm Queen had just won. A tremendous roar went up at Victoria Park. I tried to keep calm but it was difficult."

The following season, 1966-67, Storm Queen returned to trounce the males in the Caulfield Guineas and beat all-comers in the George Adams (now Emirates) Stakes and Lightning Stakes, all Group 1 events. In the same racing year, he produced Galilee to win four Group 1 races and multiple feature-race winners Fulmen, Lowland, Gay Poss, Century, Dayana, Tontonan and Taj Rossi soon followed (all within the next seven years).

There's no doubt that the extraordinary feat of winning his first three Melbourne Cups, in succession, in the 1960s laid the foundation for his reputation, but I doubt it would have been greatly diminished had he not grabbed another nine of the three-handled loving Cups of which so many lesser trainers' dreams are made. He consistently did the impossible in a wide variety of races across the country. Nobody could match his record Australia-wide, not even Tommy Smith.

He won four Derbys with Dayana and the Perth Cup to boot. In 1973, he won an unimaginable treble with the three-year-old Taj Rossi, who claimed on successive Saturdays—the Cox Plate (2000m), Victoria Derby (2500m) and George Adams Handicap (1600m). In the 12 months between Think Big's 1974 and 1975 Cup wins, Bart won major races in the 1000m to 1600m range with Skyjack, Leica Show, Leilani, Cap D'Antibes, Martindale, Lord Dudley and Kenmark.

During the 1980s, the period of his so-called drought between Hyperno's 1979 Cup win and Kingston Rule's triumph in 1990, Bart still managed to win 63 Group 1 races. Not only did he resurrect the unpredictable and injury prone Hyperno to win the Cup, he also claimed the Australian Cup and Rawson Stakes with him. He prepared Ming Dynasty to win a second Caulfield Cup at seven, and he dominated the 1986 and 1987 seasons with Beau Zam, Campaign King and the 'coat hanger' Sky Chase and confirmed his penchant for a 'surprise' feature Flemington Straight Six win with Elounda Bay, Foregone Conclusion, Hula Chief and Taj Quillo.

From the 1990s on, he not only won the Cup on five occasions but deployed that magic touch to ensure that Shaftesbury Avenue, Let's Elope, Saintly and So You Think were very nearly unbeatable—with the middle two each being named Horse of the Year. It was a title claimed nine times by Cummings-trained runners, only three of them were Cup winners.

For all his success, Bart insisted it wasn't plain sailing from day one.

"Until I brought my own horses I was doing

He consistently did the impossible in a wide variety of races. Nobody could match his record, not even Tommy Smith.

no good at all," he said on his 79th birthday in 2006. Cummings was licensed in 1953 and waited five years for his first Group 1 winner—Stormy Passage in the 1958 South Australian Derby.

But 1958 was more significant, as that was the year he first went to New Zealand to buy horses. "That was the start of it," Cummings recalled, "in the next few years there I was able to buy horses like Galilee for 3200 guineas and Red Handed for about 1800. That was the turning point for me."

"Galilee was turned in front and walked like Charlie Chaplin but I liked him. Roy Higgins, one morning, thought he'd broken down at the trot but once you got him on to the course proper he went from Tin Lizzie to a Rolls Royce," Cummings said.

So how did he do it? How did he select these and the dozens of top-class horses that followed? No, it wasn't genius, said the man himself in that 2006 interview.

"You get a hunch. You get a sixth sense, I suppose. First of all you've got to have an eye for a horse and powers of perception. Remember what you see and never forget it. Remember what you saw in those good horses you bought in the past, remember over 30 or 40 years. Then provided the pedigree supports what your eyes see, you can proceed. But you have to identify the likely good stallions early, before the fashion catches and the prices go too high.

"Then just be patient and feed them well. I suppose the most important thing becomes the feeding. I've always stuck to the old-fashioned way: mix my own feeds; separate grains; focus on a high protein diet. Some feed supplements are good, but you can't rely wholly on the prepared feeds. Tommy [Smith] had a similar means of feeding and I believe Gai [Waterhouse] has followed Tommy," Bart said.

Even if the secrets of the 'eye' and the feed mix were never fully revealed, the Cummings' training legacy will live on, not only through son Anthony and grandsons James (who took on the team on the death of his grandfather) and Edward (foreman to his father, Anthony), but also through the trainers on the remarkable list of men who, at one time, worked for Bart. They include John O'Shea, John Wheeler, John Thompson, Steve Richards, Nigel Blackiston, Guy Walter, Shaun Dwyer, John Miller, Leon Corstens, Dave Edwards, Danny O'Brien, Joe Hall, Ron McDonnell, Murray Johnson, John Morish, Guy Lowry, Lord Huntington, Matthew Smith and Kevin Ryan.

"A few repeat offenders there, but they were mostly pretty good fellas," said Bart in his inimitable way. "The ones who asked all the questions turned out to have the most ability. John Wheeler, Guy Walter, Leon Corstens did very well….and Dave Edwards."

STEPHEN MORAN has been writing about the racing game for more than four decades, was the first racing editor of The Sunday Age, a commentator on the deceased TVN, and a former editor of Best Bets.

MEETING ROYALTY: It was Golden Slipper day, 1966, and the Cummings-trained Storm Queen had been backed to win a fortune in the 2YO Classic, the tenth running of what has become one of Australia's big four. The family money was on with Bart's brother Pat, one of the big punters of the era. The SAJC had made a special request for Cummings to stay in Adelaide as his champion Galilee was long odds on to win the feature event of the day, named for the Queen Mother. As the presentation was being made, the crowd roared as Storm Queen stormed home to victory at Rosehill in Sydney. In the background, as Cummings greets the Queen Mother is jockey John Miller.

Bart—
in his own words

DANNY POWER made his way through the archives to trace
the life and times of Bart Cummings, all in Bart's own words.

I wouldn't care where the next horse came from,
he'll win the Melbourne Cup. He'll kill 'em at the
end of two miles …

That brash, confident statement was made in *The Sporting Globe* in August 1953, under the head 'Welloch past the post'—not, as you would expect, by the young, ever-confident Tommy Smith, but an even younger trainer without a Group 1 win to his name, Bart Cummings. It's hard to believe, more than 60 years later, that this was same taciturn, private, one-liner champion we came to know, but Bart it was, referring to the four-year-old stayer Welloch, on the Melbourne Cup trail. It's almost impossible to find a similar quote of such outrageous confidence from Cummings, especially after he hit the big time in the 1960s when he trained three consecutive Cup winners.

Call it the exuberance of youth in the spotlight for the first time, but one thing is for sure, it was made without the pressure of his father, Jim, who was on holidays, sternly watching over his shoulder.

Cummings, then aged 26, took over the training of Welloch late in the 1952-53 season after his father left Australia for an extended holiday in Ireland.

After the Jim Cummings-trained First Scout won the Goodwood Handicap (1200m) at Morphettville in May 1953, a few days after Cummings snr took his break, the South Australian stewards stepped in and demanded Bart, then in caretaker mode, take out his own licence.

The most important horse in the team was Welloch, who had finished fifth in the 1952 Cup as a three-year-old, and was high in the betting markets for the 1953 Cup. His young trainer was clearly keen to impress.

Young Cummings trained and campaigned Welloch until just before the Caulfield Cup— he finished fourth behind My Hero—when his father returned and all the Cummings horses were transferred back into his care. Welloch didn't "kill 'em"—he went on to finish ninth behind Wodalla in the Melbourne Cup.

Bart Cummings had to wait another five years to have his first Cup runner; the flashy chestnut Asian Court, who finished 12th behind Baystone, a week after winning the Werribee Cup (2100m).

Even by then, the young trainer had learned to be reserved when fronted by the press. After Asian Court won at Werribee he said: "He probably won't run in the Cup, I doubt he stays beyond 12 furlongs. It's a bit silly to bother accepting, but I will. Maybe he will show me something over the week to warrant a start." Asian Court was unplaced. Cummings' fame was still a decade away, but his reflections had already piled up.

KEPT THE FAITH:
In a changing era, when video screens became the way to watch racing—whether in the trainers' room, or on the big screen—Bart kept to tradition, using binoculars to track his charges. Veterans of the turf will recall when this was the only way to follow the field!

THE EARLY YEARS

"If you ask me to pinpoint my start in racing, you'd have to say I drifted into the sport rather than set out to become a trainer. It was more of a hobby to fill in the time. I developed an affection for the horses Dad trained and overnight the hobby changed to an obsession."

"When I left school I took off on all types of work. I sold clothes behind a counter and mustered sheep on an outback station. It was all part of gaining experience of human nature. You've got to know people as well as horses if you want to become a successful trainer."

ON HIS FATHER (1974)

"Old dad was terrific. He used to pick them and breed them, and nobody took much notice in those days."

"All we ever spoke or did was horses. Dad was thin, straight up sort of man, very serious, very religious. Mum was quiet, always called me a 'fair little devil'. Dad was a strict man, I was always getting orders from him, but things he told me I remember and use. If you follow in your father's

footsteps you're at a tremendous advantage, you hold on to his ideas, even when you change them, and Dad was of the old school."—1975

"My grandfather, Dad's father, was a battler, trying to grow wheat in a place that was practically without rainfall. It was rough. When Dad was about 16, an old uncle wrote to him to come up and help work his station near Alice Springs; told Dad he'd be his heir, and the uncle was around 80. Well Dad worked for a couple of years, then took a look at the old boy and said to himself, 'He'll see ME out'. So he took off. His pay for the two years' work was two horses and a lead-pony. For three solid months he rode and grazed them, down the empty middle of Australia, about 1000 miles to Jamestown. He was in luck, there was good rain, and the Mitchell grass was high. Those horses hit Jamestown with dapples all over them. There was only one setback. The first time those horses ever saw a bike, it was a feller riding a penny-farthing up the main street of Oodnadatta. They panicked they cleared off, with Dad chasing them following a trail of saucepans and stuff that fell off their packs. After that, he by-passed the towns."

ON HIS WIFE VALMAE (1974)

"Like a good filly she caught my eye."

"We met in the barn dance. We went to the same church, and church dances. Val liked the races, which I guess was just as well. She enjoyed a modest bet, picking in some ridiculous woman-way that made no racing sense at all. But she'd win—more often than I did. We got married a year later."

[And Val on Bart, 1975: "He's got a driving will to win. It's bred in him. And he's good at organising others, better really than doing things himself. He was a bit of a playboy. They called him the Black Prince. His mother and dad used to worry, but I don't think they realised how much he was absorbing."

And…"All this success, it's been so gradual. I don't notice any real change, though of course it's there. Mostly, I'm battling to see Bart's success doesn't impinge too much on the family life. Anyway, first up, he worked for his dad, and yes he was a strict man. But he gave us six horses and a stable to train them, and that was the beginning."]

REFLECTING IN 1968

"It was terrific. We thought, fancy winning a Melbourne Cup … my, how's this. Then we did it three times to prove it wasn't a fluke."

THE THEORIES (1975)

"Modern day methods of correcting the imbalance in a horse are essential to get the best

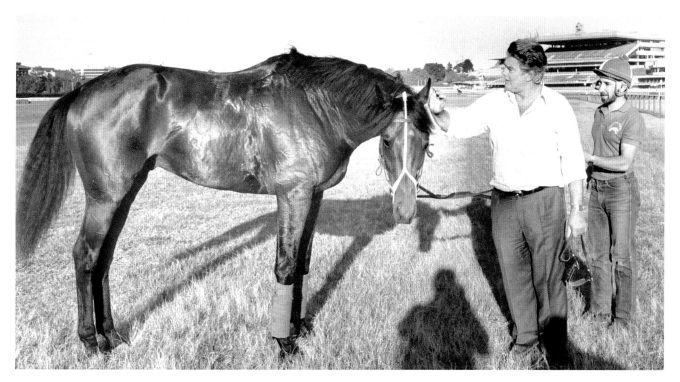

out of the animal. Owners are up for a lot of money to race horses nowadays, and it is essential to determine as quickly as possible the limitations of each horse. Once a deficiency is discovered, and cannot be corrected, I am obliged to tell the owner. After all these methods have been applied on humans in hospital for the past 40 years."

"The idea is to get them jumping out of their skins. Only then can you program them successfully for an upcoming season."—1978

KEEPING TRACK

"It's not easy. Every horse is worked and written up in a day book and this information is indexed on individual business and health cards kept from the time a horse is broken in until it retires. The business side details the financial side, race performance, time, track conditions, owners and colours. On the health card all pathology tests and treatments are noted, x-ray reports and maturity tests. I keep track of every horse by watching the cards and when I see them I reassure myself from appearances. A good horseman can judge a horse's condition by just looking at it, just like a butcher judges meat on the hook."—1978

[This system was in place from 1963, when the stable grew to levels requiring such meticulous record taking.]

"Application and concentration on the team is the secret of success in this business and as a trainer you can't afford to let any detail slip while getting a horse ready for the track."—1978

[In 2009, Cummings wrote his biography, with the assistance of the journalist and author, Malcolm Knox. On Cummings' death, Knox

wrote in Fairfax Media of one of their meetings, in which the cards were discussed.

"Can I make a copy of one?" I said.
"Why?"
"For the book. It would interest people to see how you go about it."
Bart reached across and snatched the card away.
"So—that's a no?"
"They're secret," he said. "I don't want any other trainers knowing about them."
"But," I thought how to put this gently, "they're just common sense, aren't they?"
He nodded, as if I'd finally got the point. "That's why we can't show anyone. Common sense. Nobody else has it."]

WORK BEFORE PLAY

"I love a game of tennis and I might make it on to a golf course twice a year—should play more. But if you take a day off in this business you need two to catch up. You have to stay in there and have everything in your mind—what the horses are doing, how they are working, if they are eating well."

BART THE PHILOSOPHER

"The horse has to want to race, it has to have the will to win—and I usually know when it does. The more you work with the horse, the more you understand them—therefore you make your own luck, I suppose."

"You never stop learning in this business. The more you listen the fewer mistakes you make. There's an old saying. *'The wise old owl sat on the oak. The more he heard, the less he spoke. The less he spoke, the more he heard.'* We should always be like that wise old owl."

HORSEMAN FIRST AND FOREMOST: Bart was often quoted as saying the secret of his success was a mix of patience and common sense, treating each horse as an individual, with individual needs. But there was more to it than that. He had the eye: the eye to choose a champion from a field of yearlings, and the eye to see what a fit racehorse needed to produce his best. Here he casts an eye over the imported US stallion Rosedale, with track rider Joe Agresta. Rosedale finished third to Kensei in the 1987 Cup.

AFFECTION APLENTY: Roy Higgins came to Melbourne as a skinny apprentice in the late '50s, but by 1965 he was up there with the best, and he needed every ounce of skill and power to drive Light Fingers (pictured together post-race) across the line to beat Ziema in a bobbing finish. He would do it again for Bart in 1967, again driving his mount Red Handed to win narrowly from Red Crest. Pundits reckoned that without Higgins neither would have won. Years later at a function, Higgins and Cummings (who by then had won 12 Cups) shared the stage. Said Higgins: "If it wasn't for me you'd have only won 10 Cups." Replied Cummings: "If it wasn't for me, you'd have won none."

"Horse nature, human nature, there's no difference. We all need to be loved. We go better with a pat on the back than a kick in the tail."

LOVE AND UNDERSTANDING OF THE HORSE (1975)

"I like to see them going around … I like to see them cantering … doing strong pace work"

"When Light Fingers was at a full gallop her head and tail were nearly on the same line. It makes the jockey look as though he's sitting high, but he isn't.

"When you get a good mover, a grass cutter (points to photo of Tontonan), it's a great thing to see.

"The horse isn't thinking right which means he hasn't got the will to win. He doesn't sleep well and he doesn't travel well.

"You can walk in on some of ours when they are lying down in a box and they won't get up, because they know you aren't going to hurt them.

"A lot of horses don't take the whip either. They go much better hands and heels. This is usual with a brilliant non-staying sort of horse. For some reason stayers seem to handle the whip better."

"You try harder to patch up a good horse. If that doesn't work, the horse must be put out for a spell and nature left to take its course."

JOCKEYS

"I realise that a top rider affects the price, but the first concern is to win, and that's were they come in."—1966

"I stick to the top riders. I don't often mix socially with jockeys, I don't think many trainers do."—1974

"I like a jockey with not a short rein … a long rein …(Peter) Cook's got a good long rein, so has (Roy) Higgins and Glynn Pretty. You shorten up a horse and the harder you make him pull."—1975

"I give fewer instructions (to jockeys) than other trainers. I put the best jockeys on my horses and leave the riding to their own initiative. How could you tie down Bill Williamson or Roy Higgins with instructions when no one knows what will happen from the start of a race?"—1975

"A jockey must use his initiative in a Melbourne Cup. But, of course, a rider in just one or two seconds can ruin six months' work in planning by being impatient or showing poor judgment."—1975

"It's all a matter of reflexes; quick thinking and cool judgment. I want my Cup jockeys to be physically fit and mentally relaxed. If they are worried before a race, then you are in trouble."—1975

"The worst jockeys are the ones who tell you how to train, what's wrong with the horse and this and that. The best advisers are the track riders that work with you … some are better than veterinarians. They get off and say, 'not quite right in the off front (right leg)'."—2008

EVEN PATIENCE HAS ITS LIMITS (1978)

"If they (horses) haven't shown you something by the time they are four, there is not much hope for them."

FLEMINGTON V RANDWICK (1979)

"There are no better racecourses in the world than Flemington and Randwick, but Flemington is the only place to prepare a horse properly for a Melbourne Cup. Randwick's training tracks are far too busy for a Melbourne Cup preparation.

It's almost impossible to prepare a horse for 3200 metres when there are 11 or 12 horses swishing past on the track every morning. Such conditions make your stayer pull against the jockey and the horse becomes unsettled and impatient. Horses are more content and happier in the slow gradual routine at Flemington, which is a lot quieter than Randwick. It's a matter of environment."

THE IMPORTANCE OF GOOD STAFF (1975)

"A good horse and a bad strapper is a poor combination."

"If a bloke is going to kick the Khyber out of a horse because he has tread on his toes, the horse is going to be shrivelling up into a corner."

"I'm a perfectionist in anything I do. If I delegate authority, I like to follow it up, and make sure it is done."

YEARLING SALE SELECTION (1975)

*Not all faults are bad, Cummings said.
He's forgiving of some faults, if he likes the horse.
For example, Galilee was pigeon-toed but it didn't
concern the trainer.*

"I look for things I like in yearlings and I don't make exceptions on some points. It didn't worry me that Galilee was pigeon-toed, but I wouldn't have bought him if he was turned out. If you want a perfect horse, you could wait a lifetime and miss out."

"The most important thing is selecting the right horse. There is no substitute for speed … a slow horse is a slow horse."

Athleticism "A heavyweight boxer doesn't make a long-distance runner."

"Light Fingers and Leilani, the way they were built they were physically able to carry weight over a long distance."

"I never worry too much about a yearling who is narrow in front. You usually find horses that are widest in front are half-mile jobs."

Pedigree and conformation "Even eating habits, temperaments are passed on. In selection, the breeding come first, and you vary the training accordingly. You have to learn when *not* to work a horse, and when not to race it. I'm more interested than most in the maternal line, but there's a look, too."

"Conformation has to be right, and size plays a part … it's the way they look, the way they stand and move and work, it's a rhythm about them, the way everything matches together, so they won't use up unnecessary energy."

RESPECTED RIVALS:
The great trio of trainers in a rare photograph together. From left it's Colin Hayes, Tommy Smith and Bart. Said Bart of the two rivals: "Both are good organisers with big teams and big turnovers. Tommy Smith was a good competitor… always a constant irritation though. Colin Hayes was the same—to a lesser degree."

LOVING A STAYER (1974)

"I get a lot of satisfaction out of stayers. The thing is not to know when to race them, but when *not* to race them. You've got to be patient enough not to race them."

TRAINING FILLIES (1975)

"When you get a good filly, don't subject her to too much hard work and she'll look after you."

"I never work Leilani with another horse, she's too competitive … she'd use up too much energy."

BETTING

"If a trainer bets too much, he loses his judgment."

MAN OF FEW WORDS

"I am only free with my words when I do my block."

ON TOMMY SMITH AND COLIN HAYES (1974)

"Both are good organisers with big teams and big turnovers. They are very competitive and Smith his having a great season."

"We live in different worlds really. I crack a joke with them, but there's no need to go dancing with them."

In 2003 (with a laugh): "Tommy Smith was a good competitor … always a constant irritation though. Colin Hayes was the same—to a lesser degree."

ON GAI WATERHOUSE

"Gai's following a similar pattern to her father, gets a lot of publicity and hype, gets the results though."

ON LEE FREEDMAN (1995)

"They say Freedman copied me— he's a good judge."

IRRITATED BY SPEED (2014)

"I think there should be a 2000m race and a 2400m run every couple of weeks or so. Then the country went mad on sprinters when the Golden Slipper was introduced (in 1957). Before that, when I first started training, there was only five races run over five furlongs (1000m) on the eastern seaboard each year. Now there is one every day—it is over the top, absolutely ridiculous."

ON BOOKMAKERS (2014)

"Our racing is better than in Europe. Too many bookmakers there. The best racing is in Japan and Hong Kong. They have the best prizemoney in the world and they have no bookmakers. The TAB is where we get most of our (racing industry funding) money from and if we look at Japan and Hong Kong, why can't we do the same. There is a pattern there for us to follow."

ON PASSING THE BATON

"He (Anthony, then 21) worked with me for 12 months, but is now back at university doing a business management course. It's something I did not have, so we'll see what he can do with it."—1978

ON HIS GRANDSONS, JAMES AND EDWARD (SONS OF ANTHONY) 2013

"The grandsons are going well. They ask questions and that's what you want them to do. James is getting there, he works hard and is good around horses. Edward's a natural.

ASTHMA IS THE ONLY THING DAD EVER GAVE ME (ANTHONY CUMMINGS 1992)

"He's probably right."

AFTER HIS THREE-MONTH SUSPENSION (1979) OVER LLOYD BOY'S POSITIVE SWAB

"I was quite shocked at the outcome, I wasn't ready for a holiday. It takes a lifetime to build up contacts and then you are wiped out. A suspension means that a trainer cannot carry out his occupation; you lose contact with your owners, although many of mine said they will stick with me whatever happened. Things like this just make you try harder. I've tried hard all my life and this is another challenge. I'll take it on the chin and come back bigger than ever."

ON TRAINING (1976)

"I was only struggling along in the early years. After a while when you wake up to it, you sort of get the idea of it all, it all comes easy then."

"I think patience is the biggest thing with horses, not to rush them. Don't push them too hard after a race, let them recover. One horse might take 24 hours to get over a run, another 10 days. Let nature adjust things as it will. Try to push nature, and you are going to bust something. The horse will break down, you are going to strain a heart, he's going to bleed or strain a blood vessel."

ON WINNING

"You never get tired of winning. There is no substitute for winning, especially when you consider the alternatives."

"I don't know about breaking records. You never make any money looking back; you only make money looking forward. It's what you haven't won that you need to aim for. You can't live on past laurels. You can't get a quid looking at the past."

"I've made a lot of friends in racing. They're a wonderful group of people in racing. They're good winners and they're good losers; they're not all mercenary."

"There's an old saying, it's not the money in the sport that counts, but the money helps … it helps keep the wolf from the door."

OUTSIDE THE SQUARE (1978)

"A weight-for-age Caulfield Cup is not such a silly idea."

SIX CUPS—ON BREAKING ETIENNE DE MESTRE'S RECORD (1977)

"Never in my wildest dreams when I started training did I think I would break this record. It's certainly one of my proudest moments …"[Although he added: "This is all in a day's work for me."]

THE NOBBLING OF BIG PHILOU (1969)

"I feel very sorry for the people who backed Big Philou for the Melbourne Cup because they did not get a fair go. Our horse has been interfered with by a person or persons unknown to us and because of this a lot of money has been lost to a lot of people. I know I am splitting straws, but in a racing sense there is a big difference to a horse being doped and being given a purgative."

In 1970: After a lengthy inquiry Cummings was cleared of any wrong doing.

"I am please my side of it is over. I don't like to be tied up in these cases. Security at my stables is as good as any at Flemington."

THINK BIG BEATING LEILANI IN 1974

"I've beaten myself."

ON THINK BIG'S ORDINARY 1975 CAMPAIGN

"You can't just give up when you have a real two-miler in your stable—there just aren't many around."

THE AUSTRALIAN BREEDING INDUSTRY (1967)

"We also import a number of good stallions, but some of our best broodmares are sold to America because of the economics of business. I would like to see us bringing (importing) more broodmares."

A MATTER OF PERCENTAGES (1974)

"People ask what I get out of it … well, it's 10 per cent of the stakes."

"My answer to my critics—and I don't think I have many—is that I liken myself to a stock agent who may sell $3 million worth a bloodstock in a week. His percentage would be equal to a trainer's percentage for 12 months work … after all I am only operating on a percentage of results. Any trainer who is dedicated to his profession and leaves no stone unturned in the welfare and feeding of his horse could not possibly make a profit out of training fees alone. It is well known that Tommy Smith and I show thousands of dollars loss on training fees. I rate the cost of my stables in various states at about $250,000, and the wages bill about the same, so I am dependent on the 10 per cent of stakemoney to offset the loss in

GRANDSONS:
The line will continue through Bart's son Anthony Cummings, and then through his grandsons, Edward (left) and James. Bart and James formed a partnership in 2013, and James will continue to train Bart's team. Edward is foreman for Anthony's team, just as Bart was for his father, Jim.

PERFECTION:
Bart always rated Saintly at the top of his list of champions, perhaps because he also bred him, and shared in the ownership. "He is a magnificent horse," he said. "I bred him, we named him, I part-owned him and trained him, and we loved him." Photographed here after the 1996 Cup, with jockey Darren Beadman. Saintly returned in the following autumn to win the WFA Orr Stakes (1400m) at Caulfield, but broke down and never raced again. He lives out his days at Cummings' Princes Farm.

stable expenditure before making a profit. I also manage broodmares for my clients and analyse pedigrees for them."

"The stakemoney on offer allows the average trainer and jockey to make a living without resorting to supplementing their income through betting. I know from my experience that that (betting) doesn't pay."

THE INTERNATIONALS

In 2007 when only three overseas horses had won the Cup—Vintage Crop (1993), Media Puzzle (2002) and Delta Blues (2006).
"Maybe they could start making the Cup an invitational race and simplify the number of overseas runners to five. That's what they do in Japan, and we have to be invited to compete in places like Hong Kong. It will probably be a good way to go because eventually our prizemoney will continue to be so much better than overseas. We pay down to $80,000 and if you finish midfield it basically pays for the overseas trip."

In 2012, after imports Americain, Dunaden and Green Moon had won the Cup.
"It is much easier for the foreigners to qualify. They can win a $5000 Listed race overseas and that's enough for them to get into the Melbourne Cup. It is becoming very one-sided and it is obvious they are pandering to the internationals. If they keep going like this, we will have to 'spot the Aussie' in the Cup."

ON SAINTLY (2013)

"He is a magnificent horse. I bred him up at Princes Farm, we named him, I part-owned and trained him, and we loved him. He won the Cox Plate and the Melbourne Cup that spring. That was quite something, pretty memorable, really."

ON SO YOU THINK (2012)

"Perfection on four legs, I couldn't put it any better than that. You don't get any better than him, he is the finest, most genuine horse I have ever trained. And I've trained more than I can remember. If he had stayed here, he could have

"I was doing much better without these blokes. They came to me."

"My business has not collapsed, it is just another challenge. Life's full of challenges and I've faced worse. I should be able to sell all these yearlings by Christmas. I have been left carrying the can, but even if it takes one, two or three years or whatever, I will win my way around."

THE COMEBACK (1990)

"Yeah, we're in front. We've got some nice horses, the stables are terrific and I believe there are some potential champions. Of course, what I'm looking towards in the Melbourne Cup. Everyone wants to win the Melbourne Cup, and I haven't won one in a while."

ON OWNERS (2008)

"You've got to be a politician, you've got to be salesman, you've got long hours, you've got to understand human nature. It's very, very difficult and you've got to have a bit of sense of humour, otherwise you'll go nutty (laughs) and take it too seriously."

ON WOMEN IN RACING (1967)

"I'd rather see women in mini-skirts than jodhpurs."

ON LUCK (1975)

"If I've been lucky it's just that I have been fortunate to train good horses. There is one thing about good luck, it might turn on you one day."

won four Cox Plates, not two … His nature and will to win were his best attributes. It was a great shame to see the Australian racing public miss him so early in his career."

ON AIDAN O'BRIEN (2012)

After the Irish trainer admitted he got the training of So You Think wrong when the horse arrived in Ireland and apologised to Cummings:
"Apology accepted. I'd like to congratulate him. He's a slow learner and I'm glad he picked up at the finish."

THE MONEY TROUBLES (1989)

When Bart Cummings' "Cups King" syndicates failed to attract investors by June 30, 1989 … the accountants pulled out of the venture.
"When the going got tough they left me holding the bridle."

He said it had taken him 30 years to reach the top of his profession, and despite his wealth had five children to support.

AND LAST BUT NOT LEAST

"If the horses couldn't gallop you would never had heard of me"

"You can never spend too much time looking after horses. You could spend 24 hours a day with them and it still wouldn't be enough."

"I'm a fatalist, if I win or lose, it is all in a day's work."

"I like what I am doing, I think that is why I get some success out of it. If someone enjoys their work it makes a difference."

"Let's face it, I like horses."

To Ray Thomas (Daily Telegraph) 2013.
"I'm just an ordinary sort of fellow … can train a bit though."

Sources: The Sun-News Pictorial, The Herald, The Australian, Herald Sun, Daily Telegraph, Women's Weekly, Inside Racing, The Story Of The Melbourne Cup— Australia's Greatest Race, The Modern Melbourne Cup.

The Cummings formula

DANNY POWER had many conversations with Bart Cummings through the years, and was able to draw from him his Melbourne Cup winning formula

"To win the Cup one day" is a common thought for anybody connected with Australian racing, whether trainer, jockey, owner or strapper; and after Comic Court had won in 1950, strapped by a young Bart Cummings, that same thought went through Bart's mind. He recalls he said to himself that day: *"I'd like to win the Cup myself one day."*

Cummings not only made winning the Melbourne Cup his mission, but also he made winning the great race an art form. In a spread from 1958 (Asian Court was his first runner) to 2014 (Precedence, in his fourth appearance), Cummings prepared 88 runners for 12 winners and 10 placegetters with a remarkable five quinellas. Nobody comes near him. Lee Freedman and Archer's trainer Etienne de Mestre are next best with five Cup winners. Cummings' strike rate of runners to winners is even more remarkable—14 per cent— no wonder the odds were always shorter when JB Cummings was next to a runner's name.

In his latter years (from 2008, on the eve of his 81st birthday, to 2014) and with the VRC paying out prizemoney of a minimum of $125,000 (from sixth to 10th place), seven of his 12 starters took home some cash, including a winner (Viewed) and a placegetter (So You Think).

The Cup in 2008 was the 50th anniversary of Cummings' first Melbourne Cup runner—Asian Court— something that had slipped Bart's mind for many years.

Cummings had often stated that Trellios (sixth in 1959) was the first horse he started in the Melbourne Cup— even Cummings' excellent website (*www.bartcummings. com.au*) wrongly credited Trellios, not Asian Court.

I had been researching his runners through dusty archives, and armed with the knowledge Asian Court was his first, I asked him about his first Cup runner. "Trellios in 1959," Cummings replied. When I suggested that it could have been Asian Court in 1958, Cummings pondered a few seconds. "Asian Court, yes, you're right. He won the Werribee Cup the week before and we backed him!"

Asian Court had earned his Cup place by winning the Werribee Cup (then run over 2600m) six days earlier, but didn't give the young trainer a glorious start. The gelding struggled to run the two miles (3200m) before finishing 12th to Baystone. The same year his father, Jim, had his last Cup runner—Auteuil (ninth).

Asian Court, a son of Comic Court and also raced by Comic Court's owners, the trio of Lee brothers, was a 40/1 chance to win the Cup. Cummings said the horse he recalled as "the chestnut with the white blaze" was best at distances around 2000m, so he wasn't expected to win at Flemington. No matter, the stable's pockets were full from Werribee. "We got 9/1 at Werribee," he said. The memory doesn't fade on the important issues.

The following year, Trellios, a genuine top class weight-for-age galloper, went into the Cup as one of the favourites at 7/1. Cummings already was showing his talent for planning, as Trellios was weighted on only 7st 7lb (47.5kg), yet Cummings ran him in non-penalty weight-for-age events and along the way the horse gave Cummings his first Group 1 win in Melbourne by winning the Underwood Stakes (1800m) at Caulfield. Trellios earned his Cup run by winning the Mackinnon Stakes (WFA 2000m) on Derby day. Ron Hutchinson rode the gelding into fifth place behind Macdougal, the horse he got off to ride Trellios.

Cummings did not have long to wait to live his 1950 dream. He won his first Cup in 1965 when the wonderful little mare Light Fingers, ridden by Roy Higgins, nosed out her stablemate Ziema. The following year Cummings took back-to-back quinellas in the Cup, when the great stayer Galilee beat Light Fingers, and in 1967 Higgins rode Red Handed to win, giving Cummings three Cups on end, and the legend was born.

He had watched the way his father had trained stayers, and applied his own theories and experiences to the task. I asked him whether there was a formula to it. Like most things with Bart it was simple, consistently held, and based on common sense, aptitude and experience:

Cup horses must have raced over at least 10,000 metres in their lead-up races in the spring.

It is important to have run in at least one race over 2400 metres or further.

It is essential to race on Derby day, three days before the Cup, in either the Group 1 Mackinnon Stakes (WFA 2000m) or the Group 3 Lexus Stakes (2500m). Even after 11 years without a Cup win, Cummings used his formula to peak Kingston Rule on the day to win the trainer's

WORKING TOGETHER:
Bart was one who kept his foreman for long periods, and in many cases they would leave his fold and become successful trainers in their own right. Here is is photographed with long-time Melbourne foreman Leon Corstens, after the 1991 Cup win of Let's Elope.

eighth Cup in 1990. Kingston Rule had seven lead-up runs in that campaign, covering 13,423 metres, and Cummings topped him off with a second in The Dalgety (now the Lexus) on Derby Day. He followed a similar pattern with Let's Elope in 1991—the mare won the Caulfield Cup and Mackinnon Stakes (on Derby day) before her Melbourne Cup win, beating stablemate Shiva's Revenge.

Less known, is Cummings' preference to gallop his contenders on Cup eve (over 1200m), and again on Cup morning (over 400m at 15 secs to the 200m), despite the fact they may have raced on the Saturday.

And there is that famous Cummings mantra: "The cheapest thing in racing is patience and it's the most seldom used, so I do it the cheap way—plenty of time Aand patience. That's paid off for me handsomely."

But it's more than patience that made Cummings a racing legend. Vital was his ability to choose young horses—he had the eye for a staying horse from their earliest months—and the skill and the timing of a master horseman to get his runners right on the day.

"You need a horse with a staying pedigree that has a good turn of foot, and has a good constitution, and a trainer capable of teaching the horse to relax," he said. He was renowned for the calmness and relaxation of his stable complexes. "Keep their energy in reserve for race day," he said.

All Cummings' Melbourne Cup winners followed the rules except for Light Fingers (1965) and Saintly (1996). Saintly was the only one to run in the Cox Plate rather than the Caulfield Cup. As it was only 10 days between his Cox and Cup assignments, Cummings said there was no need to run again on Derby day.

Saintly completed the other "tasks" of his trainer's job list—he had run 11,540 metres in lead-up races, and finished second in the AJC Metropolitan Handicap at Randwick, which was then run over 2600 metres (now 2400m).

Light Fingers was treated differently from the others because of her small size, the fact she was a mare, and had suffered an interrupted preparation. Light Fingers won the Craiglee Stakes (WFA 1600m, Flemington), but she was injured in the Caulfield Stakes (WFA 2000m) and missed the Caulfield Cup. Her lead-up run was in the Mackinnon Stakes (2000m), in which she finished third to Yangtze.

The stoutly bred Light Fingers (by Le Filou from Cuddlesome, by Red Mars, the same cross as Cummings' 1967 winner, Red Handed) ran only 7000 metres in lead-up races to the Cup, and she didn't compete in a race over 2400 metres.

"She was a little, light mare, who didn't need as much. Leilani (second to Think Big in 1974) was the same," said Cummings, who once described Leilani as having the "figure of a ballerina".

Leilani won the Caulfield Cup by three lengths on a light preparation. She was penalised very harshly with 3.5kg in the Melbourne Cup, and finished second to her stablemate.

Yet Leilani still fitted the criteria. She ran in races totalling 10,600 metres, won the Caulfield Cup (2400m) and also won the Mackinnon Stakes (WFA 2000m). It was a "light" preparation in that Cummings was easy on her between races.

Like a painter putting the finishing touches to a masterpiece, the Hall of Fame trainer worked all his Cup horses on Cup eve, and again on Cup morning. It was easy, sharp work to "put the sprint back into their legs".

On Cup morning, the Cummings-trained contenders stride up 400 metres. They leave the track eager, snorting and prancing for more. It is a method Cummings had no intention of altering.

"It is perfection plus, why change it? It's like in cricket; when you are taking wickets you don't change the bowler," he said.

For all the theory, he knew the importance of horsemanship—that innate ability to understand the animal and its needs. "The horse has to want to race, it has to have the will to win—and I usually know when it does. The more you work with the horse, the more you understand them— therefore you make your own luck, I suppose."

And, he knew the value of watching, learning from his own success and the success of others. This philosophy is part of the Cummings display at Victoria's Racing Museum, written on a plaque: "You never stop learning in this business. The more you listen the fewer mistakes you make. There's an old saying, 'The wise old owl sat on the oak. The more he heard, the less he spoke. The less he spoke, the more he heard'. We should always be like that wise old owl."

Cummings was concerned about the future, as the Australian breeding industry changed, with less focus on the staying horse, and on patience. He believed it was becoming increasingly harder to find suitable Melbourne Cup-style horses at the yearling sales, putting some of the blame on the shuttling of stallions.

"The shuttle stallions from Europe … are a lot softer boned but I have noticed that when those stallions stay here, and don't shuttle back to Europe, from their second crop the horses are far more mature and better boned," he said.

"It is a proven fact that the sun in Australia and New Zealand, and the calcium in the ground, creates better bone. Calcium without the sunshine doesn't have the same effect.

"If a stallion stayed here and got a full 12 to 18 months of sunshine, he would be a lot better sire. Both he and his progeny will improve.

"When Leilani's sire Oncidium arrived in New Zealand (to stand at Te Parae Stud), he was light-boned, and tight in under the knee. In 18 months he grew three quarters of an inch of bone (20mm) that made him a normal type of stallion for our conditions.

"Lord Howard (de Walden) who was on the committee of the Jockey Club in England, and who had originally owned Oncidium, was in the mounting yard at Flemington when a horse by Oncidium won. He came up to me and said he can't believe that his stallion was producing horses like that. He sold Oncidium thinking he was not much chop.

"I go to the yearling sales with three things in mind. The Golden Slipper, the Derby and the Melbourne Cup. You must set your goals high. And if they don't make it they might win something in the bush." Indeed they might, but very few left the bright lights of the city, other than in their learning period.

On the following pages, STEPHEN MORAN reviews the Cup winners, from Light Fingers (1965) to Viewed (2008)

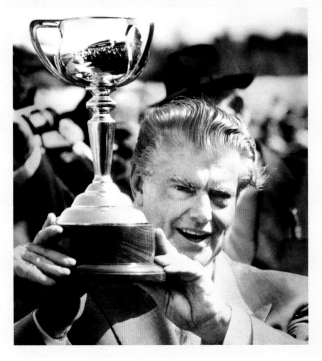

A tried and trusted formula

1. Cup horses must have raced over at least 10,000 metres in their lead up races to the big race.

2. One of those races must be over 2400 metres or further.

3. It is essential to race on Derby Day, in either the McKinnon or the 2500 metre handicap; each of these events provides a guaranteed place in the Cup field.

4. Ensure the starters have a hit out on Cup eve and again on Cup morning.
And, don't attempt the impossible: "A heavyweight boxer doesn't make a long distance runner".

A THING OF BEAUTY: Kingston Rule, the 1990 Cup winner, was regally bred, a son of the super champion Secretariat and the multiple Group 1-winning mare Rose Of Kingston. The breeding stood out with his racetrack performances—he set the Cup race record, a time yet to be beaten—but also in conformation and beauty, as clearly shown in his photo.

1965

LIGHT FINGERS

A day for the ladies

Everybody's darling Light Fingers seemingly did not have the physique nor the preparation to match it with the boys in the 1965 Melbourne Cup. But she simply put such trifles behind her the year that London model Jean Shrimpton shocked the ladies and delighted the boys in her Derby day outfit of a sleeveless shift (of then mini length) without, glory be, gloves, hat or stockings.

"She's quite a nice looking filly but she is very small," was Cummings' original assessment of the filly by Le Filou. It's not known what he said, or thought of Shrimpton at the time. However, in his 2009 biography *Bart: My life*, he wrote that "he only had eyes for one female that day and she wasn't a two-legged one". He was into the female form, however, describing Light Fingers as having "the figure of a ballerina".

Light Fingers was a sister to The Dip whom Cummings' dad Jim had trained to win the 1962 The Metropolitan (2600m) in Sydney. Jim Cummings had come out of retirement, at the age of 76, in November 1961, after Bart had been 'rubbed out' for 12 months after a form reversal win of his horse Cilldara who had been backed from 33/1 into 7/2 in a minor event at Morphettville. The horse improved as Cummings had used the then novel blinkers for the first time on him, but the politics of the time over-ruled that simple and logical explanation.

Stature aside, Light Fingers was an obvious Cups candidate having won both the VRC and AJC Oaks at three. She also had the pedigree to run the trip, by the French stallion Le Filou from the Red Mars mare Cuddlesome, a cross that provided Cummings with another Cup winner, Red Handed, two years later.

Despite all that positivity, Light Fingers was a 15/1 chance to win the Cup after her spring preparation had been twice interrupted— by illness and injury. Her success was arguably the first real insight into the ability of the man who nursed her through a post-Craiglee Stakes virus and a post-Caulfield Stakes ricked shoulder. A shot of cortisone in her sacroiliac by the legendary vet Percy Sykes may have helped.

Higgins doubted his mare could reach Ziema, especially after a scrimmage caused her severe interference 1000 metres from the line, forcing her back to midfield: "Light Fingers was not giving as much as I had hoped and I felt that lack of racing might be telling, but she found new life over the final 100 yards. She is only a pony, but she has a heart as big as herself. She is a great mare."

Miller too, thought he would win the race at the clock tower, but, he said, "He just could not see out the two miles. He would have won by three or four lengths if he had continued his run right to the line".

Light Fingers was just the sixth mare to win the Cup and with 8.4 (52.5kg) she was the highest-weighted mare to win (a record since eclipsed by Empire Rose (1988, 53.5kg) and then Makybe Diva (2004, 55.5kg; 2005, 58kg). With jockey Roy Higgins extracting every ounce from the tiny mare, she beat stablemate Ziema (John Miller) by a nose and Cummings became just the fourth trainer to quinella the Cup*. Light Fingers was nicknamed 'Mother' by Higgins. He said she was so mature that she mothered other young horses in the stable and was so tractable she could be used as a lead pony of older horses'—provided they weren't grey. "She hated grey horses," Cummings wrote, "she even went out of her way to bite a clerk of the course's pony." Good thing Ziema was black.

TIGHT:
Light Fingers, on the
outside, just nabs
her stablemate Ziema.

LATER:

"She was remarkable," Cummings mused more recently when asked about the first of his Cup winners. "We only walked her for 10 days before the Mackinnon Stakes (in which she finished third, in a classic Derby day run for a Cummings' Cup runner) after she was galloped on in the Caulfield Stakes."

Light Fingers returned in 1996 and carried a hefty 57.5kg to run second to Galilee; this time, the jockeys were reversed. It was a Herculean effort given that Makybe Diva was given 2.5kg more, in 2005, after winning the previous two Cups.

Light Fingers was, rightfully, included in the VRC's *Greatest Cup Never Run* field which marked the 150th anniversary of the race in 2010. She was the 22nd inclusion in the field and joined three other Cummings Cup winners—Galilee, Saintly and Think Big. She was placed 16th in the phantom race that, in

this writer's opinion, demeaned her. She was much better than that! Then again, it was a field of great champions, with Phar Lap 'outlasting' Carbine, with Makybe Diva a short distance away!

Roy Higgins insisted Light Fingers was the best horse he rode. "She could win first-up over 1000m or a Melbourne Cup. I always had trouble trying to find one better than her," he said. (Higgins died in March 2014.)

Pat Bartley wrote, in his biography of Higgins (*Roy Higgins: Australia's Favourite Jockey*), "It is telling that in later years he refused to have any more than a few modest pictures in his house of any of the horses he rode, but he proudly displayed a large one of Light Fingers."

*Trainers to quinella the Cup before 1965 were Harry Robinson (1920, Poitrel, Erasmus), James Scobie (1900, Clean Sweep, Malster) and William Forrester (1897, Gaulus, The Grafter).

 *1966*

GALILEE

Not a racehorse, 'an express train'!

Galilee, widely acclaimed as one of Australia's greatest stayers, took home the 'new' money in 1966, around $41,000 in the year when decimal currency was introduced in Australian and the median house price in Melbourne was $9700.

John Miller, on Galilee, took his revenge on Roy Higgins (Light Fingers) from the year before with the son of Alcimedes, the 11/2 favourite, beating the 12/1 defending heroine by two lengths in front of 82,000 fans.

Miller said after the race: "I never dreamed I'd get the chance of winning the big one again." Higgins remained loyal to the mare who would remain his lifetime favourite: "Galilee was better on the day, but she's the best racehorse."

These were two very fine racehorses. Both were later included in the notional best Cup field ever. Galilee had the good horse's winning strike rate of 50 per cent (18 wins from 36 starts, four of them rated Group 1 in that era) while Light Fingers was very close to that mark with 15 wins from 33 starts (three G1).

Galilee, after running second in the Epsom Handicap in Sydney, returned to Melbourne for the 1600m Toorak Handicap and came from last on the turn to win decisively. And yet he was 14/1 the following Saturday when he won the Caulfield Cup with 54kg.

Galilee was a star but opposed to a brighter one in Tobin Bronze, who was the odds-on (8/11) favorite for the Caulfield Cup after winning the Liston, Craiglee, Underwood and Turnbull Stakes that spring. He was entitled to be favourite for the hallowed Caulfield 2400m handicap just as the up-and-coming Galilee was to be shorter than double-figure odds. But then, the retrospective view is always sharper

It seems the punters had not yet learned to fear Bart Cummings. Cummings said he drifted (from 6/1 to 14/1) in the market as some punters thought he was limping after the Toorak Handicap and that unfounded rumours spread that he was injured—all a consequence of the way he walked which fooled many an observer and a few participants, including Higgins, and earlier, at the NZ yearling sales, the redoubtable Tommy Smith, who quipped to Cummings that he had bought a dud.

Tobin Bronze finished sixth behind Galilee in the Caulfield Cup. Miller was suspended until Derby eve for causing interference, on the home turn, to Tobin Bronze, who then went on to win the Cox Plate and the Mackinnon Stakes (and the Caulfield Cup the following year). Miller put in a 'cold ride' third aboard the strong finishing Galilee in the Mackinnon. He was questioned by stewards but escaped sanction. Cummings was among the many trainers accused of using the Mackinnon as a 'practice' or warm-up race for the Cup. For the record, eight Cummings Cup winners ran in the Mackinnon for two winners—Let's Elope and Rogan Josh. Four others—Light Fingers, Galilee, Red Handed and Gold And Black—finished in the first four. The two one-paced stayers Thing Big (in 1975) and Viewed (2008) were well beaten. Make up your own mind.

In the Cup itself, Galilee carried 56.5kg (1kg less than Light Fingers) and sustained a long, late run to overhaul the brave mare with The Metropolitan winner Duo a half-head back in third place.

Only The Trump, in 1937, had been able to do what Galilee had done: win the Toorak, Caulfield Cup and Melbourne Cup in the same year.

LATER:

"This ain't a bloomin' horse, he's an express train," jockey Miller said of Galilee after his amazing performances in 1966 and 1967.

After Cummings' death, rival trainer Gai Waterhouse—in her stable blog—listed her top five Bart moments. She rated the 1966 Melbourne Cup as number one.

Gai wrote: "The 1966 Melbourne Cup was one of the greatest ever run. The Cups King won the race with the champion Galilee, and one of the great mares of the 20th century, Light Fingers, ran second. What sets this quinella apart is the fact that Light Fingers after winning the previous year's Cup, was asked to carry 9.1 (57.5kg). This is almost the same weight that Makybe Diva carried in her third Cup win. So for winning half as many Cups as the Diva, Light Fingers was asked to carry much the same weight. This just shows how good Light Fingers was ...

"But the mare had to give weight to Galilee and he is one of the top five greatest stayers to run in Australia. Bart got the best out of both horses and both will be remembered as all-time champions. Galilee is perhaps the third best stayer (out-and-out stayer) Australia has seen behind Peter Pan and Carbine.'

In the October edition of *Inside Racing,* Gary Crispe, Australia's *Timeform* representative, rated Galilee Bart's best, ahead of So You Think, Century and Taj Rossi, with Saintly (6th) the next best of the Cup winners, with Hyperno , 11th, Let's Elope , 12th, Viewed 13th, and Light Fingers, 16th. Cummings, in his autobiography, wrote: "(Galilee) was the best horse of that era and the one I think could be the best horse I've ever trained and one I had selected myself as a yearling." He had picked out the colt while inspecting yearlings at the Trelawney Stud, near Cambridge in New Zealand's north Island, in the January of 1964.

An indication of Galilee's greatness can be gained through the subsequent feats of Tobin Bronze, beaten by Galilee in the 1966 Caulfield and Melbourne Cups and also in the Fisher Plate on the final day of the 1966 Cup week. Tobin Bronze won nine races after going down to Galilee in that Fisher Plate, including seven now with Group 1 status: the Doncaster, All-Aged Stakes, Toorak Handicap, St George Stakes, Orr Stakes, Caulfield Cup and Cox Plate.

BEST OF THE BEST:
Galilee is rated by *Timeform's* Gary Crispe as the best of the greats from the Cummings yard. Here, jockey John Miller acknowledges the applause of the crowd as he returns to scale on the champion after the 1966 Cup, led in by owner Max Bailey. The pair had missed by a nose in 1965, when Bailey's Ziema lost to Light Fingers. Miller said he never believed he would have another chance at victory after missing out on Ziema.

1967

RED HANDED

The champ had a head 'like a violin case'

It was Bart, and 'The Professor', Roy Higgins, again in 1967 with Red Handed, 4/1 equal favourite (with the unplaced General Command), rallying late under Higgins' urging to beat the New Zealander Red Crest (Ron Taylor) by a neck. Many felt that Higgins had got the better of the Kiwi, Taylor, but he was no mug. In 1964, Taylor, then 23 and out of New Zealand for the first time, had won the Cup aboard Polo Prince with a great, ground-saving ride even if *The Waikato Times* could be no more generous than reporting that "a handy ride by Taylor" contributed to the win.

Red Handed's win was Cummings' first moment of history in the Cup—it was the first time a trainer had saddled up the winner three years in a row; by then The Cup had been run 106 times.

Cummings had high hopes for Red Handed, by Le Filou and bred on similar lines to Light Fingers (by Le Filou from a Red Mars mare), in 1966 but he fell in the Geelong Cup a fortnight before the Cup and fractured a bone in a hock. Thus, he was sidelined from October that year until August 1967 when he won first-up down the straight 1000m track at Victoria Park. As Red Handed was resurrected, Light Fingers had been retired and Galilee succumbed to a splint on a bone on a foreleg.

The first real display of Red Handed's high quality came when he ran second to the mighty Tobin Bronze in the Toorak Handicap, and again in the Caulfield Cup despite coming from barrier 20. Red Handed was doing his level best to emulate Galilee and while he had come up one place short in the lead-ups, he went into the Cup having escaped any penalty.

Tobin Bronze progressed to his Australian farewell at Moonee Valley, rapturously applauded by 37,000 at the Valley as he won his second Cox Plate before leaving for the USA where he finished third in the Washington DC Laurel International on debut and later won four races without ever really taking to dirt racing or the northern hemisphere climate.

Red Handed progressed to the Mackinnon Stakes where he finished fourth behind another great weight-for-age performer, Winfreux. That was enough to have him a public elect for the Cup and he ground out a tough win after looking to be beaten at the 200m. "I thought we were beaten," said Higgins, "but then I remembered who trained the horse, and believe me, that took us both to the post." Higgins had quickly become a Cummings believer, and had become Cummings' number one rider.

A report the next morning in *The Age* noted that Cummings' mantra was already well understood, even though this was only his 13th season as a trainer in his own right. Noting that Red Handed had missed almost a year's racing, *The Age* reported: "Cummings displayed one of his greatest attributes—patience". And patience was the one philosophy that Cummings would always espouse when asked the secret to his ongoing success. "Patience and common sense," he would say.

Red Crest, his trainer Jack Winder and jockey Taylor stayed with Tommy Woodcock—the man who had rarely left Phar Lap's side some 30-odd years earlier and who was denied a Cup of his own, as a trainer, when his much admired galloper Reckless beat all but Bart's Gold And Black in 1977. Red Crest had tender feet and the drought-like conditions in Melbourne that year did him no favours when it came to the rock-hard track condition, this well before the modern era of preparing tracks with plenty of 'give' in the ground.

LATER:

Cummings described Red Handed, rather unflatteringly, as "having a head like a violin case but he could gallop". He said: "He won a five-furlongs (1000m) race at Victoria Park (Adelaide) in August and didn't win again until the Cup. But that wasn't bad going for a horse with a club foot, a paralysed ear and a head like a violin case."

Despite that Geelong Cup injury, Cummings had a good feeling about Red Handed for the following year. "It might be asking a bit much but Red Handed might be the one for next year....," Cummings recalled he had said when interviewed after Galilee's win. "They all fell about laughing, as people often do, for some reason, when I am speaking in deadly earnest."

He also felt it was a good omen when Red Handed was stabled in the same stall as the 1890 Cup winner Carbine and Higgins insisted that Red Handed have the same bridle as Light Fingers.

This was Cummings' third Cup winner but the first to carry the stable colours of green and gold diagonal stripes, white cap, that Cummings had designed, based, he said, on his love of Australia, and had registered in 1958.

Cummings said that Red Handed was boxed for three months in Sydney after his injury before another three months of rest in Melbourne. Patience, the cheapest thing in racing but the most rarely employed, as Cummings was apt to say.

Red Handed was heavily backed when he won first-up down the 'straight five' (furlongs) at Victoria Park—Adelaide's wonderful inner-city racecourse that staged its last meeting in 2007 before redevelopment for wider public use. "Glynn Pretty was riding and he told all his jockey mates that Red Handed was a special," Cummings recalled.

That win was a forerunner to what would become a Cummings trademark. His good staying horses, or horses capable over more ground, would show their mettle by winning sprint races down a straight course, predominantly at Flemington. Shaftesbury Avenue was the most notable of these at Group 1 level, but there were a raft of others who managed the feat.

To put the mid-60s Cups in perspective, jockey Taylor recalled in a 2009 interview that he earned $1800 for his 1964 Cup win and that was enough for him to secure the freehold on a property in Palmerston North.

1974-75

THINK BIG

A well-named one-day wonder

DONE IT AGAIN:
Think Big was the
champion in 1974, and did
it again the following year.
He had not won a race
between Cups, but he
had gained a new owner,
Tunku Abdul Rahman,
seen leading in the gelding.
In the background is his
friend and co-owner, Dato
Tan Chin Nam, who would
win another two Cups with
Cummings.

Tunku Abdul Rahman and Bob Hawke had a few things in common. Aside from the prime ministership of their respective countries, Malaysia and Australia, they were both tertiary educated in England, had colourful reputations for extra-curricular interests in their younger days and had a common bond as racehorse owners.

Hawke, at Oxford, was the more gifted student but the Cambridge educated Rahman—Malaysia's first prime minister—was the longer serving head of state and the more successful owner courtesy of his fortuitous 1975 Cup win with Think Big.

Rahman died, at age 87, in 1990. *The New York Times*, in its obituary, noted: "Until he returned to his homeland to begin a life of public service, he was known for his interest in poker, golf, soccer, tennis and a red sports car, not as the leader who would have the patience and skill to try to lead the ethnic Malays, most of them Muslim, and the Chinese, most of them Confucian-Buddhist, in a Government that would be at best unwieldy and at worst fraught with violence."

The Think Big story began with Cummings' better-known Malaysian owner Dato Tan Chin Nam. Cummings and Chin Nam met through jockey Glynn Pretty and Cummings said he immediately "took a shine" to his new friend who happened to be one of Malaysia's biggest property developers.

Cummings, in his ghosted autobiography, wrote that Chin Nam claimed he said to him, on their first meeting, "I want you to buy me a horse to win the Melbourne Cup".

"I told him I already had the horse he wanted. He bought a share in the Sobig-Sarcelle colt sight unseen," Cummings recalled. Chin Nam later offered a share to Queensland property developer Rick O'Sullivan as, according to Cummings, Chin Nam was "keen on a quid" and liked to spread his risks. O'Sullivan purportedly said that he was due three or four Melbourne Cups for all the slow horses he'd raced. "That's typical, you're always thinking big," said O'Sullivan's wife Joan and, hence, one story as to the name.

Long-time friend Malcolm Wuttke, who spoke at Cummings' funeral, had a slightly different version of the naming of Think Big. He said that, over lunch, Chin Nam had urged the guests "to think hard, think big" when it came to finding a name for the horse.

Think Big performed usefully as a two- and three-year-old for Cummings but his obvious promise as a stayer was generally lost, at least in the public's eye, amid the hype generated by more celebrated stablemates Taj Rossi, Tontonan, Leica Lover and Asgard. And then, in the spring of 1974, it was another stablemate Leilani, part-owned by another politician in Andrew Peacock, who dominated the racing spotlight with a commanding win in the Caulfield Cup.

The Caulfield win earned her a hefty 3kg penalty for the Melbourne Cup lifting took her weight to 55.5kg. Handicappers were tougher then, remembering that Cummings' first Cup winner, Light Fingers had set a weight-carrying record for mares, when she won the 1965 Cup with 52.5kg. Leilani confirmed her class by winning the Mackinnon Stakes on Derby day while the seemingly out of form Thing Big suddenly emerged as a Cup hope by winning the Hotham Handicap at 7/1 after a lack-lustre eighth in the Moonee Valley Cup a week earlier. Said Cummings: "We sent Think Big to Brisbane for the warmer winter climate and it did him

LATER:

Think Big failed to win again in another 19 starts after his second Cup win. Cummings often described himself and his horses as "creatures of habit". And Think Big thus: "He was good at two miles but otherwise he wasn't much good." And, for whatever reason, Think Big's habit was to come good in November and his ability to stay a strong 3200 metres was vital in an era when staying power, perhaps more than class, was the key to winning the Cup.

A gelding, Think Big lived out his days at jockey White's farm at Gisborne, Victoria. He died, at the age of 25, on February 23, 1995, and is buried at the farm.

White went on to win the Cup again in 1978 (Arwon, trained by George Hanlon) and 1979 (Hyperno) and Hyperno joined Think Big to see out his days at White's property. White's tally of four wins, matched by Bobby Lewis between 1902 and 1927, has not been bettered. White, a 2003 Racing Hall of Fame inductee, has battled multiple sclerosis late in life.

"Harry White was a great rider who excelled in staying races, said Cummings, "At his peak he was one of the best judges of pace I have ever seen."

Think Big's run of glory also marked the beginning of a life-long friendship with Chin Nam. Cummings wrote: "After his two Melbourne Cup wins with Think Big, Chin Nam had continued owning horses, but on a fairly modest scale. This all changed when I was in such deep financial trouble in the early 1990s. Even though Kingston Rule and Let's Elope won Melbourne Cups, and Shaftesbury Avenue won six Group ones, I was still digging my way out of deep, deep hole …

"When he saw this happening, Chin Nam decided to buy a lot more racehorses and send them to me. I doubt I could have got through without him." Those purchases included the 1996 Cup winner, Saintly, and Cummings' last great champion, So You Think.

good. After all, anything is better than the weather here. Since coming back his form was not so good until about the time of the Moonee Valley Cup. It was then he started to improve so much."

Leilani started favorite at 7/2, despite the severe impost, while Think Big was in the market at 12/1. Leilani looked likely to defy all, weight included, when she cruised past the Kiwis Battle Heights and Captain Peri well into the straight, but Harry White on Think Big had other ideas. "Think Big was really starting to wind up at the 300 (metres) so I pulled him out wide, put my head down and hoped for the best," White said. "I just couldn't believe it when I saw I was shooting past Leilani— I thought she was home and hosed!"

After the race, O'Sullivan apologised to those who had backed Leilani: "It would be hypocritical to say I am not happy Think Big won. But a lot of people lost their money on Leilani. I love horses, but I'm not much of a gambler."

Chin Nam was so delighted with his first foray into Australian racing that he then invited his close friend Abdul Rahman into the ownership of the horse. Cummings couldn't believe that Think Big was given 58.5kg in the 1975 Cup. That was a rise of 5.5kg on his 1974 weight and he hadn't won a race since. "Maybe the

trappings of power earned Think Big all that excess weight," Cummings said.

Think Big's 1975 spring form was poor, to say the least. He finished 10th in the Caulfield Cup, and could beat only one home in the Mackinnon, but on a dirty, dull, rainy day, he defied the 58.5kg, his odds of 33/1 and his general aversion to wet tracks to defeat stablemate Holiday Waggon, much the better fancied at 7/1, by three-quarters of a length. He was also wearing the second set of colours (green and white diagonal stripes, red sleeves), with better-fancied Leica Lover (10/1), who finished 20th, wearing the first set. Said Cummings: "No one is more surprised than I am. He only seems to win this day of the year. It is the only race he likes to win."

Think Big's victory provided Cummings with a record-equalling fifth Cup, matching the deeds of Etienne de Mestre who won the first Cup, in 1861, with Archer and four more to 1878. It was also his fourth quinella, perhaps an even more remarkable training feat. Think Big became the fourth dual winner, with Archer (1861-2), Peter Pan (1932, 1934), and Rain Lover (1968-69).

A beaming Tunku Abdul Rahman led him in, to be presented with the Cup by the Governor-General, Sir John Kerr.

1977

GOLD AND BLACK

A record broken and a Governor-General's "farewell"

Gold And Black won the 1977 Cup to give Cummings a record sixth winner. But this remarkable achievement ("It's certainly one of my proudest moments," said Cummings) was somewhat overshadowed, immediately after the race, by a drunken presentation speech from Australia's Governor-General Sir John Kerr.

And while Gold And Black started favorite at 7/2 after a slashing second in the Mackinnon Stakes on Derby day, the son of In The Purple probably had fewer people cheering for him than were supporting the second favourite—11/2 chance Reckless. Those prices were virtually reversed on the tote such was the popularity of Reckless.

Just two years after Kerr had presided over the controversial dismissal of the Whitlam Government (on November 11, 1975), he made anything but a distinguished farewell appearance at Flemington to present the trophy to the connections of Gold And Black, while waving his arms at the booing crowd like a conductor.

Dressed in the required Melbourne Cup morning suit, and vest, a red rose in his lapel, he departed from his prepared speech, staring down the baying crowd surrounding the mounting yard:

"Any little noises you may happen to hear are only static. It's just something wrong with the system.

"I want you to understand, and I know that you will, that the minor noises do not destroy the marvellous occasion today is for me and my wife …

"Life is wonderful for all of us, especially for winners of the Melbourne Cup. Congratulations

to all of you, and I'll be back as a spectator." Kerr resigned the following month. He never returned to Flemington.

Jacqueline Maley, reflecting on the Whitlam dismissal in *The Sydney Morning Herald* in 2014, wrote of the Cup speech: "His obvious inebriation, combined with his thicket of white hair and his aristocratic bearing, made him seem more like a Barry Humphries' character than the Governor-General. The crowd hissed as he tottered through his speech."

Gough Whitlam, writing in his memoir (*The Truth Of The Matter*), was even less kind: "Weaving his way down from the imperial box and making his merry remarks to the owner, the fascinated crowd and a million viewers (who) may have thought that the horse would have made a better proconsul."

Reckless was the sentimental favourite. It had taken him 33 starts before he could win a race. That and the fact he was trained by Phar Lap's strapper, the venerable Tommy Woodcock, made him something of a people's favourite. He had captured everybody's imagination, and won over the less forgiving punting souls, when he won the Sydney, Adelaide and Brisbane Cups in the first half of 1977. He was the first horse to win those three major 'two-mile' races in the one year.

Reckless and Gold And Black were well acquainted before the 1977 Cup. They had clashed in the 1976 Cup on a day when an Armageddon-like deluge played to the favour of the New Zealand mudlark Van Der Hum. Gold And Black was second and Reckless fourth. Cummings thought it may have been the one that got away:

"I was sure that without all the rain, Gold And Black would have won. We were fairly confident about Gold And Black's liking for a wet track and we liked his handicap—he was down seven kilos from the Mackinnon (which he won in '76)—but this amount of water was unprecedented.'

The two met again in the 1977 Sydney Cup with Reckless, at 20/1, beating 3/1 favourite Gold And Black by a length and a half into second place. Think Big, incidentally, was last, and sixth was Balmerino, who just six months later beat all but Alleged in the famous Prix de l'Arc de Triomphe at Longchamp in France.

Cummings spelled Gold And Black after the Sydney Cup, taking him back to South Australia. "He contracted pneumonia so seriously he nearly died. He had a lung weakness throughout his life

and he was susceptible to bronchial complaint," Cummings said. Cummings apparently wasn't brimming with confidence especially when Gold And Black was given 57kg in the 1977 Cup— a rise of 7kg on his weight 12 months earlier.

Gold And Black recovered from his illness but was unplaced in the first five runs of his spring campaign. However, his trainer was much more encouraged by his Caulfield Cup fifth to stablemate Ming Dynasty and his Mackinnon Stakes (WFA) second to Sir Silver Lad. Gold And Black looked to be on target for the holy grail; with John Duggan aboard, he had the better of the brave Reckless by a length. Duggan had finished second in the previous two Cups on Gold And Black and Holiday Waggon (1975).

It was the first taste of Cup success for Bart's

HOME AND HOSED: Gold And Black made up for the disappointment of finishing second in 1976, with an easy win the following year, driven home by Sydney jockey John Duggan.

1977

GOLD AND BLACK (continued)

son Anthony, who had just started working full-time for the stable, and for Cummings' Melbourne stable foreman Leon Corstens.

On breaking the record, Cummings said: "When I started training, never in my wildest dreams did I think I would break this record."

Cummings wrote, in his autobiography, that he said to Kerr at the presentation: "Don't get upset, sir, they're all 'commos'. It's a race meeting, sir, not a political rally. Don't worry about it." Cummings said he did not think that Kerr was drunk. "They said he was blotto but I didn't think he was too bad. He seemed quite sober to me. But perhaps I was distracted."

LATER:

Gold And Black was retired after the 1977 Cup but came back into work, 18 months later, to be prepared for the 1980 Melbourne Cup. However those plans were abandoned after he failed badly in the Sydney Cup that year.

Cummings recalled that Gold And Black then became a mount for the clerk of the course in Adelaide before being retired to a farm in Gawler (South Australia). He died in 1985 after complications during surgery for kidney stones.

Aaron Treve ('Tommy') Woodcock also died in 1985. Andrew Lemon, in the *Australian dictionary of Biography*, wrote of Woodcock's life.

"Woodcock was born on 8 October 1905 at Uralgurra, near Bellbrook, in New South Wales. In 1918 he began an apprenticeship with a Randwick trainer, Barney Quinn, riding his first winner at Moorefield racecourse in February 1922 ...

"He rode in the western districts until, aged 21 and increasing in weight, he relinquished his licence. Returning to Sydney, he bought a truck and worked as a contractor but continued to ride trackwork for Randwick trainers, including H. R. (Harry) Telford who trained Phar Lap.

In early 1928 Woodcock first encountered Telford's New Zealand yearling purchase, Phar Lap, and soon established a profound bond with the young horse that he called 'Bobby Boy'. After Phar Lap's third spectacular win, in the 1929 Australian Jockey Club Derby at Randwick, Telford

engaged Woodcock as full-time stable foreman and strapper responsible for the champion's care.

As strapper, Woodcock shared Phar Lap's celebrity status, particularly in November 1930 when he shielded Phar Lap from a gun attack three days before the Melbourne Cup.

Phar Lap's owner David Davis delegated Woodcock to train the horse for the 1932 Agua Caliente Handicap, held at a gambling resort in Tijuana, Mexico. Phar Lap's win in this, the richest race of his career, was hailed as his greatest triumph; but just two weeks later on 5 April the gelding sickened and died, in Woodcock's arms, at Menlo Park, California.

Notwithstanding autopsies, the cause of death was keenly yet inconclusively debated for decades. Scientific tests sponsored in 2008 by Museum Victoria supported circumstantial evidence that the horse died from an accumulation of arsenic, a component in legitimate tonics administered by his trainer, strapper and veterinarian. Woodcock, although unable to provide explanations, harboured a sense of responsibility and always discounted theories that Phar Lap was intentionally poisoned.

After Phar Lap's death Woodcock accepted a retainer from an American millionaire and horse breeder, Willis Sharpe Kilmer; he was obliged, however, to return home because he had contravened United States of America immigration laws. In 1934 he obtained a training permit from the Victoria Racing Club. He managed a farm at Ringwood during World War II and resumed training in 1946 with immediate success, winning the VRC Australian Cup with Knockarlow. The next year he established small stables at Mentone, relocating to nearby Epsom in 1961. Woodcock achieved success for loyal clients, notably (Sir) Reginald Ansett, Bill Stutt (a bloodstock dealer) and Dr Graham Godfrey. He won the 1959 and the 1967 VRC Oaks with Amarco (the mother of the champion Tobin Bronze) and Chosen Lady."

TAKING THE LEAD:
Gold And Black overcomes the crowd favourite Reckless and the 66/1 chance Hyperno to win. Hyperno, with new trainer Bart Cummings would make it his day two years later.

1979

HYPERNO

The horse who haunted Higgins

The 1979 Cup winner Hyperno was a triumph for Bart Cummings, who resurrected the horse after injury, but a nightmare for Roy Higgins. Hyperno was Higgins's horror horse.

The jockey, who had earlier combined with Cummings to win the Cup with Light Fingers and Red Handed, was denied this year by the narrowest margin (a short half-head) when he rode Salamander for Flemington trainer Tommy Hughes.

It was 18 months earlier that Higgins had infamously 'dropped his hands' on the leading 7/4 favourite Hyperno in the 1978 Moonee Valley Cup (run in May that year) and was nabbed on the line by 9/1 chance Clear Day ridden by Midge Didham.

The 1979 Cup story, in essence, began in November 1976. Salamander gave his first hint of staying prowess when runner-up to Unaware in a vintage Victoria Derby. Family Of Man, who would win the next year's Cox Plate, was third.

Unaware had run second to the champion filly Surround in the Cox Plate a week before his Derby win; Family Of Man had run second to her in the Caulfield Guineas. And yet neither, nor Unaware, started favourite in that Derby. That distinction went to the Cummings-trained, Higgins-ridden Ashbah, who was odds on (4/5) but could finish only ninth after, according to Cummings, 'ricking a muscle'.

Eleven days after that Derby, Hyperno won his maiden at Bendigo. He was then trained at Caulfield by Geoff Murphy and ridden by Alan Trevena. Little did Cummings know then that the NZ-bred son of Rangong and Mikarla would be his seventh Cup winner.

Hyperno was one of the first of a long list of top-class horses to win their maiden at Bendigo—giving rise to the catch cry, 'Bendigo–Nursery of Champions'. Hyperno, who would be named the 1980-81 Horse of the Year, was followed, in debut wins at Bendigo, by Better Loosen Up (also Horse of the Year, in 1990-91) and another Melbourne Cup winner Shocking (2009). Derby winners Star Of The Realm, Benicio and Don Eduardo, along with Oaks winners Grand Archway and Hollow Bullet, scored breakthrough wins at Bendigo, as did the celebrated sprinter and sire Bletchingly.

Hyperno had a reputation for being erratic and unpredictable but he trained on from his maiden to perform successfully for Murphy and, just less than 12 months after his maiden win, he finished third behind Cummings' Gold And Black in the 1977 Cup.

HAPPY DAY:
It was Cup number seven for Bart, and number four for jockey Harry White (bottom photo with Cummings), record-setters each. In the top photo, White on Hyperno (outside) appears to ask Roy Higgins on Salamander, "who won?" Hyperno's margin was a short half-head.

Cummings, in a twist, had no entries for the 1979 Melbourne Cup. His horses were entered in the name of Mal Barnes as Cummings was still serving a three-month ban after Lloyd Boy returned a positive swab to an anti-inflammatory after winning the Carlyon Cup in the autumn. Cummings, not in Melbourne at the time of the race, argued his innocence but the suspension—and that with his foreman Leon Corstens—stood. He said, when the verdict was handed down, "This is a blow to my career. I was shocked at the outcome." It was reported at the time that he added, with 'a wry smile', "I wasn't ready for a holiday." He returned to training on July 11, 1979.

Hyperno was entered in Murphy's name. The gelding had pulled up lame after running third in the Toorak Handicap in October 1978 and had raced just twice in 15 months for Murphy when Cummings took over his training after persistent overtures from part-owner Ray Lake.

Cummings was patient with Hyperno, as he graciously conceded Murphy had also been earlier in his career, but Hyperno's 1979 spring form was less than spectacular before a creditable fourth behind the Cox Plate winner Dulcify in the Mackinnon

Stakes on Derby day. "It was a pleasing trial similar to many of my Cup horses," Cummings said.

Dulcify started the 3/1 favourite in the Cup but was eased out of the race—by Brent Thomson—coming to the home turn and had to be put down after fracturing his pelvis in two places. Soon after turning for home, Hyperno cruised to the lead from Red Nose (third) and held on in a head-bobbing finish from Salamander, who had finished strongly, in the last 200 metres, on the inside of Hyperno. Higgins just missed out and White joined Bobby Lewis as the only riders to win four Cups.

LATER:

Newspaper baron Rupert Murdoch presumably has fond memories of the horse many others considered a rogue. Owner Ray Lake was to reveal that Murdoch, a friend, gave him $15,000 in cash to bet on Hyperno.

Cummings wrote of the story: "Ray didn't know where to put it (the money) safely so he stashed it in his freezer. He thawed it out on Cup morning, took it down to the track and placed it on Hyperno at about 7/1."

Hyperno won 20 races and the 1979 Cup was certainly not the end of his story. He backed up on final day to win the Queen Elizabeth Stakes, which, for the first time, had replaced the C.B. Fisher Plate on the program. Salamander had won the final Fisher Plate 12 months earlier.

Hyperno went on to win the Queen Elizabeth again in 1980, the Australian Cup and the Rawson Stakes in 1981, the Blamey Stakes in 1980 and 1981, dead-heated with My Brown Jug in the 1981 St George Stakes and ran second to Ming Dynasty in the 1980 Caulfield Cup. Harry White continued to ride him, a partnership Cummings said "impacted on the decline of my partnership with Roy Higgins". The partnership ended (later to be redeemed) in February 1980, after the pair clashed at trackwork. Cummings had engaged White for an unbeaten SA filly, Silver Shoes, a mount Higgins had expected. Said Higgins at the time: "I told Bart our arrangement was off, and I won't go back on my word. I won't even ride trackwork for him." With weight finally catching up with him, Higgins retired in 1984. White retired in 1995.

There were no fond memories for Higgins, who had declined the Cup winning ride on Hyperno whom he had described as a "bit of a mongrel". And the horse, and that moment at Moonee Valley, haunted him forever.

"Whenever I get up to speak, no matter what part of Australia I'm in, the first question is, 'how did you come to drop your hands on Hyperno'?" Higgins told Patrick Bartley in *The Age*, in 2012—in the wake of Luke Nolen's brain fade aboard Black Caviar in the Diamond Jubilee Stakes at Royal Ascot. The similarities were clear, but to Nolen's eternal relief, Black Caviar held on to win by a nose.

Higgins died in March 2014.

Lewis and White's riding record in the Cup—four winners—has but one challenger in the current crop of jockeys, Glen Boss, who rode Makybe Diva to her three wins, 2003-05.

1990

KINGSTON RULE

A blue-blood traveller

The regally and internationally bred Kingston Rule ended Bart Cummings' mid-career Cups drought when, in 1990, he won one of the most open Cups in the history of the great race.

Kingston Rule, with Darren Beadman aboard, started equal favourite at 7/1 with the Murray Baker-trained runner-up The Phantom (Grant Cooksley). Only once before had the Cup favourite started at a longer price and that was Sainfoin, unplaced at 8/1 in Tarcoola's 1893 Cup, almost 100 years earlier.

During the 1980s, Cummings had 13 Melbourne Cup runners and hardly troubled the scorer, with two thirds (Rosedale and Mr Jazz) and two fourths (My Sir Avon and No Peer) all he could yield. However, he still won a remarkable 63 Group 1 races in that decade. Not only had he resurrected the unpredictable and injury-prone Hyperno to win the 1979 Cup he also won the Australian Cup and Rawson Stakes with him in the early 80s, prepared Ming Dynasty to win a second Caulfield Cup at seven, dominated the 1986 and 1987 seasons with Beau Zam, Campaign King and Sky Chase and confirmed his penchant for a 'surprise' feature Flemington Straight Six win with Elounda Bay, Foregone Conclusion, Hula Chief and Taj Quillo. But missing the spotlight on the First Tuesday clearly stung the proud man: "The law said I was finished. There is a law that says it's better to be a has-been than be no good at all. But I was sick of being a has-been".

The Kingston Rule story was expertly detailed by Danny Power, writing for *Inside Racing* in 2011. He wrote: "Kingston Rule was equine royalty from the day he took his first wobbly steps on Kentucky's famous bluegrass. When he was born, the stud manager logged a simple report— "chestnut … magic".

"He was a product of greatness, the combining of the best with the best from both sides of the world. His sire was the legendary American Triple Crown hero and dual Horse of the Year, Secretariat, a horse that some say is the best to ever look through a bridle.

"Kingston Rule's dam, Rose Of Kingston (by Claude (ITY)), travelled across the globe, from Victoria's Mornington Peninsula, for the liaison. Her papers were stamped "champion". She was an Australian Horse Of The Year who beat the colts in the 1982 Group 1 AJC Derby, after she had won the 1981 Group 1 VRC Oaks. Her colt, with his rich, golden chestnut colouring and flashy white blaze, was everything you could hope from such a union.

"Melbourne owner-breeder David Hains, a dominant figure in Australian racing at the time, had a small, boutique broodmare farm in Kentucky to go with his Kingston Park Stud in Victoria. Hains sent a band of his best mares to Kentucky to be bred to the America's leading stallions, with the resultant offspring to return to race in Australia. It was an experiment that lasted about eight years, and included exporting Rose Of Kingston's half-sister, the 1984 Group 1 VRC Oaks winner Spirit Of Kingston (by Bletchingly), and their dam Kingston Rose (by Better Boy).

"After an unplaced run in France as a 2YO for trainer Patrick Biancone, Kingston Rule was imported to Australia and joined the stable of Tommy Smith at Randwick in Sydney. Smith and Hains had combined to dominate Australian racing earlier that decade with Kingston Town, the champion triple Cox Plate winner, who was gelded after finishing last at his racetrack debut. The same fate was on the

CHAMPIONS ALL: It's Cup number eight, and another champion for owner David Hains, who had missed out narrowly when his great champion Kingston Town was grabbed near the post by Gurner's Lane in the 1982 Cup. Hains bred both champions, and Kingston Rule would stand at stud for Hains on retirement, with moderate success.

and -bred filly Kensington Palace, who won the 1997 Group 1 VRC Oaks. Kingston Rule, aged 24 by northern hemisphere time in 2010, was then the only Melbourne Cup winner at stud in Australia. Since then, Cup winners Shocking, Americain, Green Moon and Fiorente have all undertaken stud duties.

Kingston Rule, aged 25, died at Ealing Park on December 2, 2011.

Cummings recalled that Kingston Rule was highly-strung, nervous and moody. "Someone said of him that he looked like he was expecting a tiger to jump out from behind every tree." Cummings later wrote. Cummings credited stable foreman Leon Corstens for doing a wonderful job in teaching the horse to relax.

Cummings engaged then 24 year-old Beadman to take the Cup ride after Jim Cassidy (who had ridden the horse to a great Moonee Valley Cup win) and Michael Clarke (who had won four straight jockeys' premierships in Victoria) declined to commit when offered the mount. Beadman had ridden just twice in the Cup—he was 15th on Scarvilla in 1987 and 18th on Palace Revolt in 1989.

In 1990, Cassidy finished 12th on Just A Dancer, Clarke 17th on Rainbow Myth. Steven King were the emerging stars of Victorian racing. In 1990, King finished ninth, on the Cummings-trained La Tristia. A year later he won the Cup for Cummings on Let's Elope.

Hains had clearly chosen the right man to train Kingston Rule, but he certainly had made no error in leaving the horse's more illustrious predecessor Kingston Town with Tommy Smith. Kingston Town ran last on debut in the Alfalfa Handicap at Canterbury on March 12, 1979. He was then gelded and won his next six starts. In fact, he then had an unbeaten run of 23 starts racing right-handed. Kingston Town won 30 of his 41 starts including three Cox Plates but his finest performance was, arguably, carrying 59kg into second place behind Gurner's Lane in the 1982 Cup, having been left in front on turning from home.

cards for Kingston Rule, if Smith had his way, after the handsome 4YO finished an inauspicious 35-length last in his first Australian race, on a heavy track over 1400m at Warwick Farm in May, 1989.

"That was when Hains made one of the most important decisions of his life. He had great faith in Kingston Rule and rather than geld him, he decided to spell the entire before switching trainers, and he sent Kingston Rule to Bart Cummings, the champion trainer of stayers who Hains thought would suit Kingston Rule's stout pedigree. And in one of the twists that make the bloodstock world such an interesting place, the story of Kingston Rule's lineage goes back to the master trainer from the beginning.

"Bart part-owned and trained Kingston Rose and it was Cummings who recommended Hains buy her at sale after she retired from racing. The mare was

from Sojourner, a half-sister to the flying South Australian filly Proud Miss, tracing back to the mare Opera Bouffe (a daughter of the first imported Melbourne Cup winner Comedy King— 1910), who was owned by Cummings' father Jim, and who provided Cummings senior with his first two Classic winners as a trainer—1928 VRC Oaks winner Opera Queen and 1931 SA Derby winner Opera King. Cummings claims in his book, *Bart: My life*, that he learned to ride on Opera Bouffe's granddaughter Cushla.

LATER:

Kingston Rule broke down after three starts in the autumn of 1991, and was retired to stand at Hains' Ealing Park Stud, Euroa. From limited support, he sired eight stakes winners from about 190 winners, including the outstanding Hains-owned

1991

LET'S ELOPE

A great romance

Let's Elope competed through a golden era of Australian racing. Rarely, if ever, have as many outstanding horses graced our tracks at the same time. Better Loosen Up, Sydeston, Super Impose, Rough Habit, Prince Salieri, Shaftesbury Avenue and Naturalism head a list of stars, a list that is anything but exhaustive.

Thus, her performance to win seven consecutive races (four at Group 1 and three at Group 2 level) between October 1991 and March 1992 ought to be praised even if her trainer had beaten the handicapper when she won the Caulfield Cup with just 48.5kg and the Melbourne Cup with 51kg. However, any doubts about her class were dispelled when she returned in the autumn to win the Orr, St George Stakes and the Australian Cup.

Let's Elope, an imposing chestnut mare by Nassipour from Battle Waggon's daughter Sharon Jane, was described in 1992 by the much respected racing writer Bill Whittaker as "having a stride reminiscent of the peerless Bernborough".

Let's Elope, so named as the dam of her grandsire was Runaway Bride, was one of two Nassipour yearlings purchased by Melbourne pedigree enthusiast Roy Fleiter at NZ's Trentham saleyards in 1989. The other was Lord Revenir, who won the 1991 The Metropolitan at Randwick before finishing fourth behind Let's Elope in the Caulfield Cup and 13th behind her in the Melbourne Cup.

In the meantime, Fleiter, who raced the mare with his wife Dorothy and son Tony—general manager of Dalgety Bloodstock—had sold Let's Elope for $NZ150,000, as a late three-year-old in June 1991, to Melbourne businessmen Dennis Marks and Kevin White. Selling a $16,000

LOPING AWAY: Let's Elope took all before her in the spring of 1991 and the following autumn, winning the Cup in a canter, and completing the Caulfield-Melbourne Cup double. She later had some success as a broodmare, producing Stakes winners Ustinov and Outback Joe, the latter winning the 2014 Adelaide Cup over the Melbourne Cup journey of 3200m.

yearling for $150,000 seemed like good business and her original trainer Dave O'Sullivan, while recognising her staying talent, had told the Fleiters he didn't think she was up to Cups or weight-for-age class. O'Sullivan was a highly accomplished horseman and he was compensated, that very year, with a Cox Plate win at Moonee Valley with Surfers Paradise.

The Fleiters, later, graciously conceded that O'Sullivan's opinion may have been clouded by the fact that most of Let's Elope's early racing and trackwork had been on wet tracks which she clearly did not relish. Each of her seven wins, in that extraordinary run of Group races, came on tracks rated fast.

Let's Elope was not among the original entries for the Cup, which had closed on June 4. A new late entry clause had been introduced. Late entries, costing $1000 (10 times the original fee) closed on June 18, and the then VRC handicapper Jim Bowler recalled that the mare's entry and payment arrived with just minutes to spare. "She was the last horse entered," Bowler said.

She was beaten in her first three spring runs for Cummings, but those runs were on softish ground. He first appearance on firm ground was in the Turnbull Stakes. She was greatly advantaged by the 'set weights plus penalties' conditions and with a 9kg advantage—she was able to thrash the ever reliable Prince Salieri by almost three lengths. Such was her rate of improvement that, a month later, she beat Super Impose and Prince Salieri at weight-for-age in the Mackinnon Stakes.

Either side of that, of course, she won the two Cups. Her margin was narrow at Caulfield but decisive at Flemington where she had two-and-a-half lengths to spare over stablemate Shiva's Revenge, making for Cummings' fifth quinella in the big race. She and jockey Steven King, celebrating his 22nd birthday, then had to survive a protest from Shane Dye who rode Shiva's Revenge. The first Cup protest of the century was dismissed but King was later suspended for six weeks, which was the toughest careless riding penalty imposed by Pat Lalor in his then 12 years as chairman of stewards in Melbourne.

"She had a great constitution,' Cummings said of Let's Elope, "and provided the track was dry, I thought she was a good thing in the Cup." So did the punters: she was sent out a 3/1 favourite, the shortest-priced winner of Cummings' dozen.

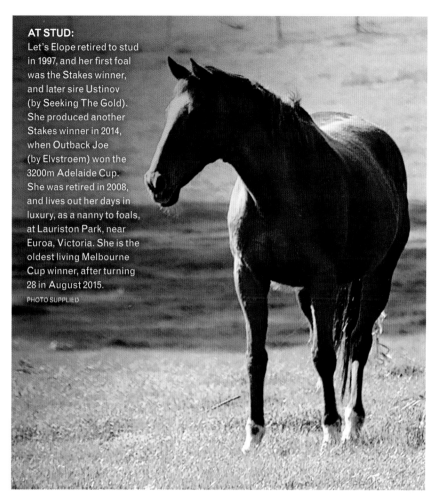

AT STUD:
Let's Elope retired to stud in 1997, and her first foal was the Stakes winner, and later sire Ustinov (by Seeking The Gold). She produced another Stakes winner in 2014, when Outback Joe (by Elvstroem) won the 3200m Adelaide Cup. She was retired in 2008, and lives out her days in luxury, as a nanny to foals, at Lauriston Park, near Euroa, Victoria. She is the oldest living Melbourne Cup winner, after turning 28 in August 2015.
PHOTO SUPPLIED

LATER:

Cummings later said he doubted he had trained a better mare. "Leilani and Light Fingers are the only ones who bear any comparison," he said.

Let's Elope suffered a strained near-fore sesamoidal ligament after winning the Australian Cup in the 1992 autumn but recovered quickly enough to compete through the 1992 spring. She beat Better Loosen Up in a much-publicised $75,000 winner-take-all match race, the Super Challenge at Caulfield, in October. That was Better Loosen Up's seventh run after his almost year-long lay-off with a bowed tendon, and Let's Elope's second run after her ligament strain.

Both horses went on to the Cox Plate, surely one of the best ever. "She made it to the post but she wasn't fully fit," Cummings said. Nevertheless, with Greg Childs aboard, she finished a head second to the evergreen Super Impose, but was relegated to fifth on protest.

Despite the strength of that year's race, Naturalism started evens favourite after winning the Memsie, Feehan and Turnbull Stakes, but it was not to be as he and Sydeston unseated their riders when they were unable to avoid the fallen leader Palace Reign, who appeared to lose his action and tumble for no apparent reason.

Let's Elope progressed to the Japan Cup later that year in which she bled and finished seventh on a soft track. After a mandatory three-month ban for bleeding, she was taken to the USA where she was first past the post in the 1993 Group 1 Beverly D Stakes at Arlington, only to be reegated to third for causing interference.

At stud, the best of Let's Elope offspring has been Ustinov, whom Cummings trained to win the 2001 AAMI Vase, on Cox Plate day, after running second to Lonhro in the Caulfield Guineas. Ustinov, a son of the US champion sire Seeking The Gold (Let's Elope was covered while in America), later had a moderate stud career. Let's Elope burst back into prominence in 2014, when her gelded son Outback Joe—just her fifth named foal from 12 covers—won the G2 Adelaide Cup over 3200m.

1996
SAINTLY

The horse from heaven

Some were never quite as sure about the 1996 Melbourne Cup winner Saintly as his trainer. Was Bart having a lend of us when the so called 'horse from heaven' was beaten in Sydney, as a short-priced favourite in the AJC Craven Plate and in The Metropolitan before he came south to win the Cox Plate and Melbourne Cup double?

Was he having a lend of us when he made the following comments? "I never thought I'd rate one of my gallopers up with Galilee, but Saintly was right there alongside him. If he hadn't got crook the night before the Japan Cup (just weeks after the Melbourne Cup) he would have won the race for sure. I think he would have been the best horse we've seen for a long time if he'd kept going."

Fair-minded jurors would probably conclude 'no' in both cases. Cummings had a simple explanation for Saintly's shock defeats in Sydney. His saddle slipped. "The trouble with him is that he's got a high wither and a very long barrel. When you combine that with the length of his stride it caused the saddle to slip back a couple of inches and that affected the rider's centre of gravity.

"When the saddle was positioned properly he was a different horse," said the trainer, who in Melbourne, used a wet chamois under the saddle and rubber padding under the girth strap to ensure the saddle didn't move.

Perhaps Saintly was simply better going left-handed given that he won five of his six starts in Melbourne.

Saintly was retired at four, in the autumn of 1997, with 10 wins from 23 starts. His initial strike rate had been relatively modest, with seven wins from his first 20 starts, before he closed out his brief career with his spectacular 1996 spring double and a superb first-up win in the 1400m Orr Stakes in 1997.

Legendary names of the past were distinguished by strike rates of 66 per cent plus—Phar Lap (72.5), Ajax (78.2), Tulloch (67.9), Kingston Town (73.1), Bernborough (70.2), Carbine (73.1) and Gloaming (85.1)—but those numbers probably speak of a less competitive time. Other than Kingston Town and, of course, the unbeaten Black Caviar (and So You Think in Australia only) the best of the modern era have not been able to win two of every three starts.

Saintly was part of a vintage crop of three-year-olds. A memorable 1996 AJC Australian Derby saw Octagonal beat Saintly with Filante third and Nothin' Leica Dane fourth. Octagonal had beaten Saintly in the Rosehill Guineas and the Mercedes Classic (now The BMW) that autumn but Saintly was a powerhouse when he got to Melbourne, which we first saw when he won the Australian Cup in the autumn at three.

In the Cox Plate, he scored a narrow but spectacular win from high-class performers Filante, All Our Mob and Juggler with only a half-length separating the four. Mike Hedge, writing in *Class Racehorses*, said he won "despite negotiating the home turn like a semi-trailer in a sideways skid".

The Cup was then a cruise with the Tom Cruise look-a-like Darren Beadman again on board. Saintly, an 8/1 chance, enjoyed the run of the race before coasting to a 2.25-length win from the 33/1 chance Count Chivas with Skybeau (50/1), who had run last in that memorable AJC Derby, a neck back in third place. The favourite at 4/1 was the handsome import with the wonderful British form, Oscar Schindler; unfortunately for those who fell into the mystique surrounding the apparent superiority of northern hemisphere stayers, the favourite wilted in the run home,

TRUE CHAMPION: Saintly in full flight was beauty to behold. He won the Cup hard held by jockey Darren Beadman, beating the bolters Count Chivas and Skybeau.
PHOTO COLIN BULL

finishing 15th. That superiority would take another decade to take hold.

Saintly's win was especially satisfying for Cummings for two reasons. One, Cummings had bred him. He raced and trained his sire Sky Chase and bred his dam All Grace. All Grace's great grand-dam was Dark Queen, the dam of Cummings' remarkable champion Taj Rossi and a three-quarter sister to his 1966 Golden Slipper winner, Storm Queen. And two, because he insisted he had run the horse at 3200 metres simply based on instinct.

LATER:

Cummings was to describe Saintly's Cup win as painless. "He was cantering all the way and Darren (Beadman) said he was always going to win," he said.

Saintly went to Japan for the Japan Cup, a race that had been in vogue with Australasian trainers. Horlicks (later to produce 2000 Melbourne Cup winner Brew) and Better Loosen Up won in successive years, 1989 and 1990, and Cummings had Shaftesbury Avenue run third in 1991. Lee Freedman's charge Naturalism was runner-up in 1992.

Saintly didn't make it to the post, succumbing to a race-eve respiratory infection. Eight years earlier, Sky Chase had undertaken the same trip but was ruled out with pneumonia a few days before the race. These travel-related sicknesses made Cummings very wary about travelling again.

Saintly returned for an autumn campaign and unleashed a stunning, late turn of foot to

win the Orr Stakes (1400m) first-up. "I've never seen a horse, sprinters included, gallop the last 50 metres of any race as fast as Saintly went that day," Cummings remarked.

All looked good for the impressive chestnut with the commanding stride, the horse that Cummings had dared to compare to Galilee. However, soon after the Orr, he broke down—tearing a tendon beyond repair—in trackwork at Flemington and was eventually retired to Cummings' Princes Farm. The trainer's Flemington stables would be named Saintly Place after the trainer's favourite, unfulfilled champion. Unfortunately, progress has stepped in, and this famous yard has been ripped down for apartments.

1999

ROGAN JOSH

One for the battlers

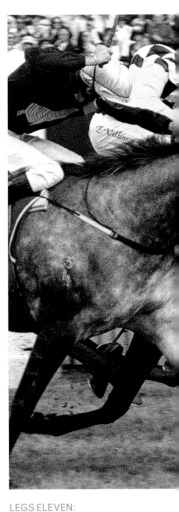

More often than not, one of the 'obvious' horses wins the Melbourne Cup. Since 1990, only three Cup winners (Viewed, Efficient and Green Moon) came off less than eye-catching last-start performances. Rogan Josh was certainly the obvious one in 1999 even if he had only recently emerged from obscurity.

His slashing fourth in the Caulfield Cup was followed by a shock win at weight-for-age in the Mackinnon Stakes and he dropped 8kg to carry 50kg in the Cup. Add the Bart factor and his starting price of 5/1 seems generous in hindsight.

The superbly named Rogan Josh, by Old Spice from Eastern Mystique, was originally part-owned by schoolteacher Wendy Green and her brother Marcus Forrest. They had bought the horse from their parents Tom and Moya Forrest, who had bred him. A hefty 17 hands, he was given time and did not race until he was four when Forrest trained him to win four of his first five starts.

Green was to eventually buy out her brother's share after a reported offer of $200,000 from Singaporean interests. After running second to King Of Saxony in the 1999 Perth Cup, (then 3200 metres) the Melbourne Cup was on the agenda and his then trainer Colin Webster magnanimously suggested that Green transfer the horse to Cummings for a 'proper' campaign.

Cummings had been in Perth for the 1999 Cup and liked Rogan Josh's pedigree. His paternal great 'grandmother' was the Le Filou mare Kind Regards, who was the dam of the high-class WFA performer Vice Regal, the granddam of Cummings' Sky Chase and the great granddam of 1998 Melbourne Cup winner Jezabeel. Cummings had had great success with progeny of Le Filou in the Cup, with his 1965 winner Light Fingers and 1967 victor Red Handed.

Rogan Josh was unplaced in his first three runs for Cummings, up to 2040 metres, but improved when he stepped up to 2400m in the Herbert Power Handicap at Caulfield, and his win there guaranteed him a start in the Caulfield Cup. His excellent on-pace fourth to the quality galloper Sky Heights in the Caulfield Cup saw his price tumble, but it dropped much, much further when he burst through late to win the Mackinnon Stakes.

John Marshall, who had not ridden the horse before, had the mount in the Mackinnon and Melbourne Cup as Cummings felt the jockey's quiet demeanour would suit the horse. Chris Munce, who had ridden him in the Caulfield Cup, was on stablemate Rebbor who finished last. Second last was Arena, ridden by Darren Gauci who had won the Herbert Power on Rogan Josh.

Prominently but patiently ridden by Marshall, Rogan Josh was able to get the better of Godolphin's front-runner Central Park to win by a half-length, It was a dream come true for owner Green, who drove from Darwin—where she was teaching—with her husband Bob to be at the Cup. And they drove back in the same Holden Commodore they called 'rent-a-dent', Cup in the back, despite Rogan Josh having earned more than $2 million for his two Cup-week victories.

Cummings and Green were interviewed Cup night by Kerry O'Brien on the ABC's *7.30 report*. Green, when asked how her family had reacted to the Cup win, said: "I think they're just overwhelmed. My husband and I have six children and they're scattered all over the world. One of my daughters is married to a man who lives in Ireland. His father rang up this morning and said, 'To be sure you're in all the papers here today…'

"My other son lives in Wales. He and his lovely

LEGS ELEVEN:
Bart's 11th Cup win was one for the battlers. He had taken over the WA galloper Rogan Josh, and had him ripe and ready on Cup Day, after the gelding had romped home with the Mackinnon Stakes on the Saturday. Rogan Josh, ridden impressively by John Marshall, beat the Godolphin hope Central Park. Despite many attempts before and since the incredible Godolphin team is yet to produce a Cup winner.
From 1998, the famous stable of Sheikh Mohammed bin Rashid Al Maktoum has tried 13 times to win the Emirates Melbourne Cup, campaigning with 19 horses (20 starters). The result is three seconds—Crime Scene (2009), Give The Slip (2001) and Central Park (1999)—and a third with Beekeeper in 2002.
PHOTO COLIN BULL

wife flew in this morning to be here. He's actually a part-owner with me of Rogan Josh.

"There's one other boy from Perth. He's here, he's signing autographs, I think. There are two of them leading the push in Darwin. I think personally my family is really celebrating. My father, my mother, they were here today. Mum and Dad led the horse back in.

"I think Dad's a little overwhelmed, to think that a little horse can come this far and be the last horse in this century to win the Melbourne Cup, and to come from such humble origins."

LATER:

Wendy Green and John Marshall, returned to Flemington on September 12 this year, to pay tribute to the 'Cups King' at a commemorative service in the Flemington mounting yard to celebrate the life of Cummings.

And Cummings' penultimate Cup winner Rogan Josh was paraded in front of the large crowd that assembled before racing began.

"From an owner's perspective, Bart Cummings was the man who delivered the dream," Green said. "He was the one who made it happen, not just for me but for many others. On behalf of all owners we thank you for that little bit of magic that changed our lives."

In a further tribute that day, the Gai Waterhouse-trained Cosmic Endeavour carried Cummings' green and gold diagonal stripes in the race named after one of his former champions, Let's Elope.

Cosmic Endevaour's owner Don Kelly (who races the mare with his wife Judy) explained: "The club approached the stable (about the change), who then rang us, and we thought it was a great idea. We jumped at the chance to wear those colours. It'll be an honour and a privilege to see her wear them in that race."

In 2013, Max Presnell, in *The Sydney Morning Herald*, recounted one of the great stories of Green's trip home, after the Melbourne Cup, with the Cup and champagne in the boot of her car.

Presnell wrote: "Green stopped off at outback settlements to share the joy with the locals, to show them the Cup and to wet the odd whistle. 'We reached Tennant Creek where I had taught some years ago,' Green related. 'There was a party involving indigenous people. We stopped and joined in.'

"Green was approached to perform a christening along the lines of what Banjo Paterson wrote: 'On the outer Barcoo where churches are few and men of religion are scanty ...'

"Lacking the necessary qualifications and holy water she declined. It was suggested the leader of a tourist bus, being close in status to a ship's captain, could officiate. Beer was offered as a substitute for the holy juice but Green's champagne was considered more appropriate.

"Alas a name for the lad was missing. Asked her preference, the mother, in the spirit of the occasion, replied: 'Rogan Josh.' And the family has a history of horse names, because Rogan Josh is the grandson of the late Phar Lap Dixon."

Green has dined out on that story in many places, across the globe, as a regular ambassador on the Cup's annual pilgrimage through Australia, Europe and Japan.

2008

VIEWED

The final glory

The 2008 Cup is memorable for many reasons: Cummings' 12th Cup winner Viewed; jockey Blake Shinn's first win at his fifth attempt; Greg Miles' magnificent call of the photo finish; an agonising second again for Luca Cumani; and the abysmal failure of the three Aidan O'Brien trained runners. And, the dramatic aftermath in the stewards' room.

It was heartbreak and heartache for many of the vanquished and heart palpitations aplenty for the winning trainer and jockey and, I suspect, for caller Miles.

"Viewed a nose to Bauer, (pause) I think," was Miles' inspired description of a finish which was perhaps the closest in Cup history. Well, at least until Dunaden and Red Cadeaux came along three years later. Miles prudently chose not to be drawn on that one.

And Cummings's heart must surely have been beating faster when Shinn took Viewed to the front with 400 metres left to travel. He was the proverbial sitting duck. No doubt too soon for the liking of the patient man. "Had he gone too early?" Cummings pondered in his autobiography, "… he hadn't waited for the clock tower…I always felt more comfortable having the last shot."

Viewed, a five-year-old by Scenic from Lover's Knot (get it? View plus Wed makes Viewed) and was owned outright by Dato Tan Chin Nam, who had shared in the ownership of previous winners Think Big and Saintly. Viewed was a 40/1 chance after running eighth, seventh, 10th and last of 11 in his four spring lead-up runs.

However, Cummings was adamant that he had no luck—with interrupted runs—in the Caulfield Cup (10th) and the Mackinnon Stakes' (11th) after an interrupted campaign. An elevated temperature forced him to miss the Turnbull Stakes and a barrier mishap ruled him out of the Caulfield Stakes. While less than confident about his Cup prospects, Cummings certainly wasn't dismissive. Despite the Mackinnon disappointment, the horse had thrived since the Caulfield Cup.

The race was oddly run, to say the least, with O'Brien's runners Septimus, Honolulu and Alessandra Volta settling in the first three spots and setting a cracking pace. The tactics were bizarre and they were three of the last four horses to finish. The three were also an odd choice as Cup candidates as each was a superior horse on soft ground.

O'Brien then had to endure the heartache and ignominy of being summoned back to Flemington, to be quizzed by chief steward Terry Bailey, after he'd already returned to his city hotel. The embarrassment did not sit well with the proud Irishman—he did not again have another Melbourne runner until 2014 when he won the Cox Plate with Adelaide, a glorious training feat.

For Cumani, who had watched the race from a distance, at the front of the mounting yard, and believed his runner had won, it was yet another empty heart. "I feel exhausted, frustrated, but determined to come back again," he said after Bauer's narrow defeat. His heartbreak was compounded by the fact that he had also finished second, with Purple Moon, a year earlier.

Cummings, who had argued—before the Cup—that the number of foreign-trained runners should be limited, was in more magnanimous mood after the race. "I feel very sorry for Luca Cumani," he said, "but it's great to see the Aussies succeed. I thought it might have been a dead-heat, it was that close."

Viewed had won by the shortest of short half-

heads, as Light Fingers and Hyperno had done.

And Shinn, who had said he was thrilled just to get a ride for the 'master', was a Cup winner. "Bart said, 'Son, just go and enjoy the moment'," Shinn said afterwards when asked if he'd been given specific instructions by the trainer.

LATER:

Viewed returned the following autumn and was winless in four starts but was placed in the Sydney autumn WFA races, the Ranvet and The BMW. In the spring of 2009, he won the Caulfield Cup—at 12/1—courtesy of an excellent ground-saving ride by Brad Rawiller.

This was one of Cummings' 18 Group 1 winners after Viewed's Melbourne Cup and one of six who saluted at generous double-figure odds—almost as if the punters had forgotten about the Cummings magic. Aside from Viewed (and not to mention Sirmione's

60/1 2007 Australian Cup win) there were: in 2008, Swick (15/1, VRC Classic); in 2009, Allez Wonder (40/1, Toorak Handicap); Russeting (18/1, QTC Winter Stakes); Roman Emperor (14/1, AJC Derby); and in 2010 Rock Classic (17/1, Australian Guineas).

Shinn's career would take a dramatic turn, in November 2010, when he was disqualified for 15 months for betting related offences.

The Daily Telegraph reported in May 2011 that Shinn was betting an average of $800 a day during a wild two-year gambling spree.

"The alarming depth of Shinn's addiction, which saw him spend $581,263.50 in just under two years on thoroughbred racing alone, was uncovered in his appeal against a 15-month disqualification yesterday.

"Stewards have previously accepted Shinn had a major gambling addiction rather than being involved in illegal riding tactics or criminal activity."

Shinn returned to the saddle in January 2012 and has salvaged his career. He had a highlight day in May of 2015 at Doomben when he rode five winners including two Group 1 races—the BTC Cup on Hot Snitzel and the Doomben Cup on Pornichet.

Viewed may have been Cummings' last winner, but two years later he had the hot Cup favourite So You Think, off a preparation that peaked at the 2040m of the Cox Plate, to finish third to Americain.

Precedence, another in the Chin Nam ownership would finish eighth in 2010, 11th in 2011, ninth in 2012, and sixth in 2014. Should Precedence, by now a 10-year-old, make the Cup field for a fifth time, when he will be the first individual Cup runner for the next generation of this famous family, Bart's grandson James Cummings.

The toughest horse of all

Long-time Cummings' foreman
REG FLEMING describes, with affection,
the track to the Cup for Viewed,
Bart's last winner of the great race.

PORTRAIT OF A CHAMPION: The photo of Viewed was taken in the days after his 2008 Cup win and is part of the Slattery Media Group's *Portrait of a Champion* series.

"Viewed was a funny story. I was sitting at home in Melbourne one day, and he raced at Rosehill and he finished about fifth over the (autumn) carnival. A lot of people don't know that Bart never won a Doomben Cup. And I rang him and said, "Bart, that horse can win you a Doomben Cup." He said to me, "He's going to Hong Kong." I said, "That's a shame. That's the sort of horse could win you a Doomben Cup."

On the Monday, Bart rings me and says Chin Nam (Viewed's owner) said if Viewed wins well, or goes good next start you can take him up to Brisbane for the Doomben Cup.

So he won a 10-furlongs race at Randwick and I got my wish, and off we went to Brisbane. We got up there and he was in a weight-for-age race and when the pace went on he just didn't know how to quicken, but he flashed home to run fifth, and Stevie Arnold (the jockey) gives me the colours and he said, "Listen, Reg, if you run this in the Brisbane Cup he will bolt in—big track, 2400 metres."

Bart was waiting for me out the back in a hire car, to drive me back to the stables. I got in the car and told Bart, and he said, "I don't think he's in the Brisbane Cup." I said, "I think he is." I rang Bill Charles and he said, "I put him in." So Bart said, "Leave him there, and we'll have a think about it." This was because he'd had eight starts this prep.

So, on Monday, we decided to run in the Brisbane Cup. He won in a canter, and that qualified him for the Melbourne Cup. Well, you've got Bart Cummings and Chin Nam— there's no way it's going to Hong Kong, is there? It's staying.

Viewed was the toughest horse I'd ever worked with. He ran in the Underwood and got crook. I went in one morning and he'd left all his feed. I took his temperature. He had a high temperature of 39.8. He was sick. So we walked him for a week, never worked him, never put a saddle on his back. So his next run was to be the Caulfield Stakes, which was two weeks away. So he went into the Caulfield Stakes, went into the barriers, and he kicked out, so they scratched him at the barrier.

So now there's a problem. This horse has gone from very ill to not having a run before the Caulfield Cup for a month. Bart and I were, on

the Sunday, at the stables and I said, "What do you think?" He said, "Listen, if we're going to run in the Melbourne Cup he's got to run in the Caulfield Cup." And his run in the Caulfield Cup, if you look at the replay, the last half furlong he was flashing along the inside.

And, in the Mackinnon, Stevie (Arnold) rode him nice and quiet and when he went to come out, our other horse, Sirmione, who had a tendency to lay in, he laid in on a horse called Rampant Lion and Rampant Lion laid in on Viewed all the way up the straight. So Viewed never got a crack at them.

So he went to the Melbourne Cup and Bart was a bit disappointed that he never got out and had a good hit-out. He just thrived from Caulfield Cup to the Melbourne Cup and me

and Joe Agresta were walking to the track on Melbourne Cup Day. We had another horse Moatize—he was having his 10th start in a race—and I said to Joe "Which one do you like?" Joe said, "Moatize." I said I liked Viewed only because Viewed was tough; he was a very strong horse. I knew when it came down to the nitty-gritty at the end of the race being the toughest horse, he would be in for the fight.

He was just the toughest horse I ever had anything to do with.

About two weeks after that race, on a Sunday, Bart rang me out of the blue and this is fair dinkum, he's laughing and he said, "Reggie Boy, I dunno how we got away with that race, I'm buggered if I do with all the problems we had, but anyway we did. ",,

This tribute to Viewed, and to Bart Cummings, was part of an interview by Helen Thomas of Cummings' long-time Melbourne foreman, Reg Fleming, on the ABC podcast 'Hoof On The Till' broadcast on Friday, September 4, 2015.

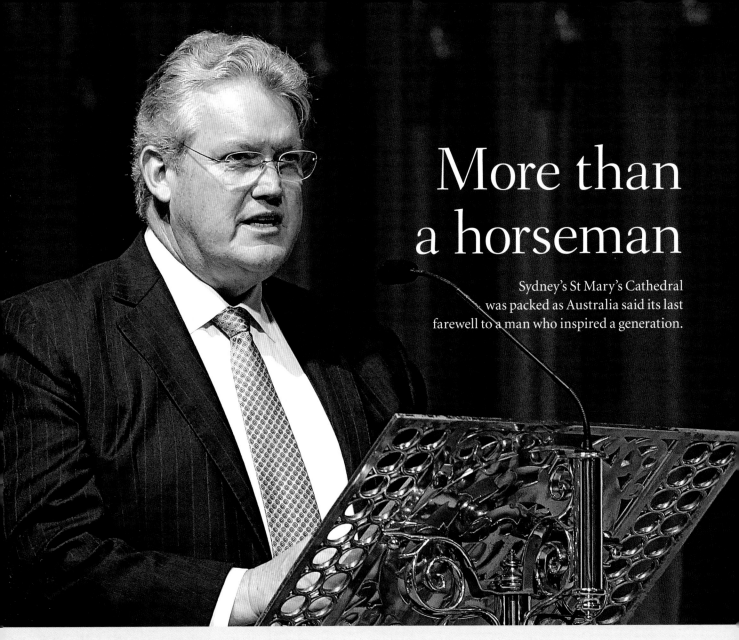

More than a horseman

Sydney's St Mary's Cathedral was packed as Australia said its last farewell to a man who inspired a generation.

unerals, they say, are not for the dead but the living; that as a species we need our moments of ritual to tame the emotional gales of the preceding days. First comes the news and numb shock, and it is always a shock, even when death is expected. Then tears, of course, and a distracting focus on the leaden business of making the arrangements. But the funeral, that's when the passing is formally acknowledged, the moment when life and legend agree to take their different forks. It is, oddly enough, an instant of acceptance marked almost as much with laughter as by tears. That was certainly the case when they buried Bart Cummings.

It had been hard at first to grasp that he was actually gone, for it was decades since Bart had seemed merely mortal. His was the presence that seemed to hover always over the Melbourne Cup—over every major meeting and carnival, for that matter—even when his horses did not collect the laurels. *Bart thinks this … Bart thinks that … Bart's not giving too much away*, which he never did. But sphinx-like beneath those bushy eyebrows, the master's opinion was forever sought and his presence revered. That was the Bart the public loved—the knowing face and twinkling eyes of a thousand mounting-yard quips. It was there again in St Mary's Cathedral on September 7, 2015, an image this time,

larger than life and on display beside the casket for all to recall; blown up and propped upon an easel to gaze with that familiar sparkle at those who mourned him, the grateful punters and legion of admirers who would prefer, always, to remember him that way.

On the other side, another portrait of another Bart—more thoughtful this image, and perhaps a better example of the photographer's art in that the face it captured was the one behind the showman's mask. There was sharp wisdom in the deep pools of those keen eyes, and a quiet satisfaction, perhaps, in the lines and wrinkles of a life lived long and well.

And at centre stage before the white marble altar, his final run through the spotlight, the coffin beneath the funerary coverings of its occupant's Catholic faith. His racing colours had been Australia's own, the glorious green and gold. But on that day, man and legend wore the sombre mahogany of polished wood and glinting silver of its handles. It was true, hard though it had been to accept. The King of Cups was dead and there was no clear follower at hand, or worthy, to ascend his throne of turf.

A state funeral for a man who was also an institution, this was what Bart deserved. There had been no complaints that an honour customarily reserved for political leaders and triumphant generals was to be bestowed on a man whose fame had been built on hay and horse sense. As the swinging censer spilled the smoke of incense and the choir's voice rose beneath St Mary's sandstone arches, the official achievements were uttered and listed. The dozen Cups, the improbable ledger of Group 1 winners, a whole life's progress from his father's Glenelg stable to the exalted peak of recognition and acclaim distilled by common usage into a single word, "Bart". That was the phenomenon whose passing warranted the presence in the cathedral of a premier, the Governor-General and a constellation of Australia's leading lights.

But there was more to him than that. There was the other Bart, the husband and father, the friend and mentor to a succession of associates who took their turns at the lectern and told their tales in his honour. They knew him not as a figure of two dimensions, the owner of that puckish face ever present in the newspapers and on the telly in the days leading up to that first Tuesday in November, but as a man in full with all the virtues, and just a few vices, the human condition implies.

> "There hadn't been a bridle made to hold him back," said Anthony Cummings. "He was more than a horseman—he was an icon, a legend, all of that; built from flames and hardship to go with success."

Son Anthony, a brumby breaker's grandson and the third of what has become four generations of Cummings boys to take up the horseman's craft, throttled tears as words spilled from lips often trembling with emotion. Real words of genuine loving sentiment and loss, they were. Yes, he conceded, his father has not always been an easy taskmaster, and there were smiles at those mentions of Bart's insistence on perfection, on having things done his way and *only* his way, of his occasional tendency to the abrasive. But now there was laughter as Anthony recalled the endorsement of the old man's latter years, how in a father's demanding estimation he "had come good". Earlier, before the Mass began, a long-ago snapshot had been shared

SOLEMN FAREWELL: Bart Cummings was sent to his eternal rest in a State funeral at Sydney's St Mary's Cathedral, on Monday September 7. His son Anthony (pictured opposite) presented the eulogy, along with Bart's friend of 50 years, Malcolm Wuttke, and racing journalist Tony Arrold.

with the congregation. It was of mum Valmae and dad (who had shared their 61st wedding anniversary two days before Bart's death) looking with approval on their eldest boy, first child of five, who was posed for the picture upon a wooden horse. How could he not have "come good" with that lineage? In the front pew, in her wheelchair and surrounded by her family, a frail Valmae dabbed at a tear even as she smiled at the memories conjured by her flesh and blood.

"There hadn't been a bridle made to hold him back," said the son, and Valmae smiled at that too.

There was more to come as friends and former employees took their turns. Bart's endearing, infuriating vagueness in regard to matters not directly related to horses also drew its share of smiles—the time, for example, he dispatched friend for half a century Malcolm Wuttke to collect an owner flying into town for a big meeting. How will I know him, Wuttke asked? "He wears glasses," said the King. In matters equine, though, no detail was overlooked. A firm believer that a winning horse is a well-nourished horse, every newly delivered bag of feed was weighed to make sure the content and balance was as the master had decreed.

The anecdotes poured forth, each fleshing out the man with little dabs of colour, every one eliciting their shares of laughter and memory.

"Dad spent time with king and queens, prime ministers, premiers and the common man, treated all equally and gave them his time", the son had said, adding that this father "was more than a horseman—he was an icon, a legend, all of that; built from flames and hardship to go with success.

"Bob Hawke described him as a great and good Australian. Enough said."

The aroma of incense was still heavy in the air as the service concluded, but that was not the dominant scent, not by any means. As they carried Bart in stately procession down the cathedral's home straight and into the perpetual sunlight of memory and legend, it was the clean air a good man leaves behind.

The VRC's farewell

Bart Cummings and Flemington were as one, not just through the Melbourne Cup—
he trained another 72 Group 1 winners at the famous racecourse. **STEPHEN HOWELL** reports.

B riefly, something was demanded of those at Flemington for the Victoria Racing Club's mounting-yard farewell to Bart Cummings— patience, the tool Bart used to say was the cheapest thing in racing and the least used.
It was just after 11.15am, the club's service was ending and any restlessness was contained as if people were waiting for one of Bart's runners in green and gold to burst from the pack in the straight and go on to win a Melbourne Cup.

Eventually, there was that burst of green-and-gold, and 268 balloons, one for each of Bart's Group 1 winners, broke free near the famous clock tower and flew towards, and past, the finish line.

On the day, the VRC paid Bart its respect in other ways, too, not the least in a green and gold walk on the lawns in front of the stands. Lines of golden paint had been sprayed on the turf to entice racegoers to file past the legendary trainer's 12 Melbourne Cup winners, from a photo post of the first, Light Fingers in 1965, through to Viewed, the last one in 2008.

Fittingly, Viewed's photo post was level with the winning post, the famous marker of Bart's Cup history on 12 first Tuesdays in November.

And on the second Saturday in September, 2015, 13 days after Bart's death aged 87, large boards of Cumming's green and gold diagonal stripes (with white cap overlaid) flanked the race meeting sponsor's boards, which flanked the line that signals the end of each race.

Bart was on track in spirit and in bronze, his statue, there since 2000 and freshly polished and presented with flowers shaped like the Cup trophy, welcoming racegoers just 30 metres of so after they came through the main gate.

Behind the statue was a memorial wall, with Bart's 12 Cup trophies displayed and a cherry tree laden with pink blossom and condolence notes. And green-and-gold flags fluttered either side of the track's big screen. If there had been room and time, decorations could also have been delivered for the other 72 Group 1 wins Bart trained at Flemington, including a remarkable 13 Australian Cups, 11 Mackinnon Stakes, eight Newmarkets, nine Victoria Derbys and six VRC Oaks. Remarkable doesn't even get close to describing such a tally.

Later, the VRC announced the overall crowd at 15,828,

and many of the several thousand at Flemington's "taste of spring" meeting got there two hours before the first race to pay their respects to the legend.

And they did so with a spring in their step as much as sadness in their hearts, catching the early trains— one at 10am, another at 10.10—and on the 20-minute trip chatting about the great man's feats at the track.

They were dressed as they would for the Cup carnival—most men in jackets and ties and many women with hats or fascinators—and some likened the early start to the anticipation of getting to the track on Cup day, when the first on the card starts at 10.30.

That was roughly the time Fr Kevin Mogg began the service, one that respected Bart's deeply religious beliefs while concentrating on the depth of his racing achievements, especially at Flemington and in its signature race, the Melbourne Cup.

Jockeys, in the colours of the Cups winners, brought forward Bart's trophies, 1999 winner Rogan Josh represented the Cup horses and John Marshall (Rogan Josh's rider) the jockeys. Marshall said during the service that 120 jockeys had won the (154) cups and eight of them were indebted to Cummings—Harry White rode three winners, Roy Higgins and Darren Beadman two— Marshall, John Miller, John Duggan, Steven King and Blake Shinn had one each.

Marshall, who also rode Cummings' stars Beau Zam, Shaftesbury Avenue and Campaign King, said he first called the trainer Mr Cummings, later it was JB.

Greg Miles, who started calling the Melbourne Cup in 1981, had to wait until Kingston Rule in 1990 to call a Cummings' Cup win, but by the end of the decade had broadcast four and he added a fifth with Viewed, in the tightest finish of all Cups.

By then it was "inconceivable to think of one without the other"—the Cup and Cummings, Cummings and the Cup.

Rogan Josh's owner Wendy Green described Bart as "the man who delivered the dream" and thanked him on behalf of all owners, especially her "unfashionably-bred crew" with their unfashionably-bred horse.

Bart's son Anthony Cummings spoke eloquently and emotionally, just as he had at the state funeral in Sydney on the previous Monday.

He talked of the Cups, saying the Flemington flagships were "only half the story" and "with Dad" it was not what horses did for him but what he did for the horses; first and foremost "feed them steak", meaning the best an athlete can eat.

"That kept him at the forefront," Anthony said. "He fed horses better than himself and, that said, took some doing …"

He described Bart's "innate sense of what's good for the horse" as his legacy.

And, in reference to one of his father's most famous comments, said that with death "he finally gets to find

out, from the only bloke who can tell him, how many flies he can have". (Cummings, once told by a council inspector that he had too many flies in his stable, asked how many he was allowed.)

Author/journalist Les Carlyon, who has written more eloquently about Cummings than any other, described him in his eulogy in the Herald Sun as "unknowable".

At Flemington he spoke of Bart the racing man, he described him as presenting himself behind a shell of deadpan humour and told the story of stable foreman Reg Fleming showing Bart and Valmae Cummings around stables in Brisbane.

Valmae saw a big cobweb and said, 'look, two spiders fighting'. After the slightest of pauses, Carlyon said: "Bart replied 'probably means they're husband and wife', and walked on."

Carlyon recalled that 65 years ago a young man rode a bay horse down the hill from off-track stables to the stripping sheds on track.

"The young man was Bart, the horse was Comic Court," he said. "It was hard to tell which of them had the blacker mane."

From strapper of his father Jim's 1950 Melbourne Cup winner, Cummings, for many years a steely grey, ended up winning 12 of his own and transcending racing and sport.

"This (the service) is a farewell to the most charismatic figure in 200 years of Australian racing," Carlyon said, adding that it was not farewell, rather the loss of his physical presence and he'd bet that in 50 years time there'd be an old man at the track telling his grandson, "I once saw Bart Cummings".

MOVING CEREMONY: Flemington and Bart Cummings were synonymous and will remain so. The Victoria Racing Club erected a statue of Bart at the track in 2000. On Saturday September 12, a large crowd gathered to pay tribute in a ceremony in the mounting yard, with the Cummings family present. Son Anthony paid tribute to Bart, and grandson James brought forward a Melbourne Cup trophy, followed by jockeys in the colours of Bart's Cup winners, each with the trainer's miniature trophy. PHOTOS COLIN BULL

Bart's 88 Cup starters

YEAR	HORSES AND PLACINGS		
1958	Asian Court 10th		
1959	Trellios 5th		
1961	Sometime 6th		
1965	**LIGHT FINGERS 1st**	Ziema 2nd	The Dip 18th
1966	**GALILEE 1st**	Light Fingers 2nd	
1967	**RED HANDED 1st**	Fulmen 9th	Ziema 12th
1968	Lowland 4th	Arctic Coast 6th	Swift General 23rd
1969	Swift General 5th	General Command 13th	The Sharper 20th
1970	Tavel 4th	Voleur 6th	Moomba Fox 19th
1971	Pilgarlic 10th	Tavel 10th	
1973	Dayana 12th		
1974	**THINK BIG 1st**	Leilani 2nd	
1975	**THINK BIG 1st**	Holiday Waggon 2nd	Leica Lover 20th
1976	Gold And Black 2nd		
1977	**GOLD AND BLACK 1st**	Ming Dynasty 8th	Vacuum 20th
1978	Panamint 10th	Vive Velours 11th	Belmura Lad 13th, Stormy Rex 20th
1979	**HYPERNO 1st**	Safe Harbour 21st	
1980	La Zap 6th	Hyperno 7th	Ming Dynasty 17th
1981	Hyperno 6th	Belmura Lad 7th	No Peer 8th
1982	My Sir Avon 4th		
1983	Mr Jazz 3rd	No Peer 4th	
1984	Bounty Hawk 15th		
1986	Empire Rose 5th		
1987	Rosedale 3rd		
1988	Round The World 5th		
1990	**KINGSTON RULE 1st**	La Tristia 9th	
1991	**LET'S ELOPE 1st**	Shiva's Revenge 2nd	Weekend Delight 22nd
1992	London Bridge 9th		
1993	Great Vintage 4th	Frontier Boy 5th	Tennessee Jack 6th, Our Tristalight 24th
1994	Gossips 14th		
1996	**SAINTLY 1st**	My Kiwi Gold 21st	
1997	Grandmaster 10th	Alfa 19th	
1998	Perpetual Check 9th		
1999	**ROGAN JOSH 1st**	Zazabelle 3rd	Rebbor 23rd
2002	Miss Meliss 10th		
2003	Frightening 11th		
2004	Strasbourg 10th		
2005	Kamsky 16th	Strasbourg 18th	
2007	Sirmione 12th		
2008	**VIEWED 1st**	Moatize 6th	
2009	Viewed 7th	Allez Wonder 16th	Roman Emperor 21st
2010	So You Think 3rd	Precedence 8th	
2011	Precedence 11th	Illo 19th	
2012	Precedence 9th	Sanagas 18th	
2014	Precedence 6th		

1965

LIGHT FINGERS

Two miles (Tuesday, November 2)
Handicap of £30,000 and £750 Gold Cup.
First: £20,650 and Gold Cup; Second: £5900; Third: £2950; Fourth: £500.

1	15-1	LIGHT FINGERS (NZ)	ch m 4y, Le Filou (FR) - Cuddlesome (NZ)	Tr: Bart Cummings	8.4	Roy Higgins
2	10-1	ZIEMA (NZ)	blk g 4y, Summertime (GB) - Najmi (NZ)	Tr: Bart Cummings	8.6	John Miller
3	20-1	MIDLANDER	blk c 3y, Centreway - Celandine	Tr: Bon Hoysted	6.9 cd 6.11	Norm Pyatt

THEN FOLLOWED:

4	33-1	Yangtze	Ron Dini		8.12	Harry White
5	20-1	Prince Grant	Tommy Smith		7.6 cd 7.8	George Podmore
6	50-1	Prince Camillo	Reg Fisher		7.8	Peter Gumbleton
7	10-1	Red William	Owen Lynch		8.6	Mick Mallyon
8	15-1	Tobin Bronze	Grahame Heagney		7.6	John Stocker
9	8-1	Craftsman	Andy White		9.5	Pat Hyland
10	20-1	Tasman Lad (NZ)	Harold Riley		8.2	Dave Cameron
11	100-1	Mission	JF Quigley		6.10	Noel Eastwood
12	100-1	Rosicombe	Mick Alessio		8.1	Fred Blackburn
13	100-1	Sir Wynyard	Bert Smith		8.7	Arthur Lister
14	15-1	Pleasanton	George Hanlon		7.8	Billy Smith
15	20-1	Jovial Knight	Grahame Heagney		8.0	Noel Mifflin
16	8-1	Strauss	J Green		8.8	Des Lake
17	4-1 fav	Sail Away (NZ)	Syd Brown		8.7	Bill Skelton
18	66-1	The Dip	Bart Cummings		8.4	Frank Reys
19	50-1	Hunting Horn	Les Patterson		8.8	Tony May
20	33-1	Dalento	Jack Besanko		8.1	Ian Saunders
21	125-1	Zinga Lee	Bill McNabb		8.11	Brian Gilders
22	66-1	Piper's Son	Morrie Anderson		8.12	George Moore
23	25-1	Algalon	George Hanlon		8.0	Ray Selkrig
FELL	14-1	Bore Head	Ron Dillon		9.1	Fred Clarke
FELL	7-1	Matloch	George Hanlon		7.13	Jim Johnson
FELL	66-1	River Seine	Neville Prendergast		8.13	Rod Dawkins

Scratched: Striking Force, Rack And Ruin, Valuate, Snowstream Lass. Won by: Short 1/2 head, 3-1/2 lengths. Time: 3:21.1. Track: fast.

Barriers: 6-1-3. Judge's numbers: 14-13-24.

PATH TO GLORY
Six starts, three wins, distance covered to the Cup: 8800 metres.

WON	18 ran	5-2 ef	David Bonney	8.8	Victoria Park	5 fur	Corporation Hcp	21-Aug-65	Diolen	0:59.7	
WON	11 ran	6-1	Roy Higgins	8.9	Flemington	8 fur	Craiglee Stakes	11-Sep-65	Nicopolis	1:38.3	
2ND	10 ran	2-1	Roy Higgins	8.9	Flemington	12 fur	Turnbull Stakes	2-Oct-65	Craftsman	2:29.7	
3RD	11 ran	2-1 fav	Roy Higgins	8.9	Caulfield	9 fur	Caulfield Stakes	13-Oct-65	Winfreux	1:48.4	
3RD	8 ran	9-2	Roy Higgins	8.9	Flemington	10 fur	Mackinnon Stakes	30-Oct-65	Yangtze	2:03.4	
WON	26 ran	14-1	Roy Higgins	8.4	Flemington	16 fur	Melbourne Cup	2-Nov-65	Ziema	3:21.1	

 *1966*

GALILEE

Two miles (Tuesday, November 1)
Handicap of $60,000 and Gold Cup valued at $2000.
First: $41,300 and Gold Cup; Second: $11,800; Third: $5900; Fourth: $1000.

1	11-2 fav	GALILEE (NZ)	b g 4y, Alcimedes (GB) – Galston (NZ)	Tr: Bart Cummings	8.13	John Miller
2	12-1	LIGHT FINGERS (NZ)	ch m 5y, Le Filou (FR) – Cuddlesome (NZ)	Tr: Bart Cummings	9.1	Roy Higgins
3	10-1	DUO	b h 5y, Double Bore (GB) – In Harmony	Tr: Ron Dickerson	8.1	George Podmore

THEN FOLLOWED:

4	25-1	Aveniam	Jack Morgan	7.13	Bruce McClune
5	7-1	Gala Crest	Ray Lawson	8.4	Peter Gumbleton
6	7-1	Tea Biscuit	Pat Murray	8.6	Hilton Cope
7	40-1	Gatum Gatum	Grahame Heagney	7.9	Frank Reys
8	16-1	Royal Coral	Bob Clarton	8.0	Paul Jarman
9	12-1	Alaska	Mo Bernard	7.12	Pat Hyland
10	25-1	Terrific	Merv Ritchie	8.1	Grenville Hughes
11	9-1	Prince Grant	Tommy Smith	9.1	George Moore
12	16-1	Bore Head	Ron Dillon	8.11	Brian Gilders
13	125-1	Dignify	Vic Moloney	7.5	Billy Smith
14	25-1	Trevors	Betty Shepherd	8.5	Athol Mulley
15	50-1	Clipjoint	Merv Ritchie	7.1	John Stocker
16	200-1	Coppelius	Brian Courtney	8.0	Mervyn Moore
17	200-1	Beau Royal	Bon Hoysted	7.2	Rod Durey
18	7-1	Tobin Bronze	Grahame Heagney	8.11	Jim Johnson
19	66-1	El Gordo	Leo O'Sullivan	7.6	Neil Campton
20	50-1	Red Brass	Grahame Heagney	7.13	Ray Selkrig
21	200-1	Mystic Glen	Fred Hood	6.13 cd 7.3	Kevin Langby
22	50-1	Winfreux	Charlie Wilson	9.2	Arthur Lister

Won by: 2 lengths, 1/2 head. Time: 3:21.9. Track: slow.

Barriers: 13-20-21. Judge's numbers: 4-2-11.

PATH TO GLORY
Nine starts, four wins, distance covered to the Cup: 12,900 metres.

6TH	17 ran	20-1	John Miller	9.0	Victoria Park	5 fur	Shakuni Hcp	6-Aug-66	Best Blend	0:58.1
8TH	18 ran	20-1	John Miller	9.0	Victoria Park	5 fur	Corporation Hcp	20-Aug-66	Redcliffe	0:59.2
WON	17 ran	7-4 fav	Roy Higgins	9.5	Caulfield	8 fur	Patrobas Welter	3-Sep-66	Manilardo	1:40.7
7TH	10 ran	25-1	John Miller	9.0	Rosehill	8-1/2 fur	Hill Stakes	24-Sep-66	Prince Grant	1:43.4
2ND	20 ran	14-1	John Miller	8.9	Randwick	8 fur	Epsom Hcp	1-Oct-66	Chantal	1:35.3
WON	13 ran	6-4 fav	John Miller	8.9	Caulfield	8 fur	Toorak Hcp	8-Oct-66	Legal Boy	1:36.1
WON	18 ran	14-1	John Miller	8.7	Caulfield	12 fur	Caulfield Cup	15-Oct-66	Gala Crest	2:27.8
3RD	7 ran	6-1	John Miller	9.0	Flemington	10 fur	Mackinnon Stakes	29-Oct-66	Tobin Bronze	2:03.0
WON	22 ran	11-2 fav	John Miller	8.13	Flemington	16 fur	Melbourne Cup	1-Nov-66	Light Fingers	3:21.9

 *1967*

RED HANDED

Two miles (Tuesday, November 7)
Handicap of $60,000 and Gold Cup valued at $2000.
First: $41,300 and Gold Cup; Second: $11,800; Third: $5900; Fourth: $1000.

1	4-1 eq fav	RED HANDED (NZ)	ch g 5y, Le Filou (FR) - Red Might (NZ)	Tr: Bart Cummings	8.9	Roy Higgins
2	20-1	RED CREST (NZ)	ch h 7y, Gigantic (GB) - Lovemorn (NZ)	Tr: Jack Winder	8.6	Ron Taylor
3	80-1	FLOODBIRD	ch g 5y, Confessor (GB) - Kaalelia	Tr: Mick Armfield	7.7	John Stocker

THEN FOLLOWED:

4	20-1	Padtheway	Jim Smith	7.9	Frank Reys
5	10-1	Prince Camillo	Reg Fisher	8.0	Peter Gumbleton
6	4-1 eq fav	General Command	Bill Wilson	8.0	Geoff Lane
7	40-1	Bellition (NZ)	George Hanlon	8.2	Harry White
8	33-1	Sunhaven	Brian Courtney	8.1	Les Burgess
9	25-1	Fulmen	Bart Cummings	8.13	Mick Goreham
10	80-1	Royal Coral	Bob Clarton	7.12	Danny Miller
11	100-1	Taunton	Ted Jenkins	7.0	Phil Alderman
12	12-1	Ziema	Bart Cummings	9.1	John Miller
13	80-1	Coronation Cadet	Noel Forbes	6.13	John Wade
14	20-1	Swift Peter	Arthur Beuzeville	7.6	Bill Camer
15	5-1	Midlander	Bon Hoysted	8.11	Pat Hyland
16	40-1	Jay Ay (NZ)	Des McCormick	8.8	Paul Jarman
17	250-1	Basin Street	Jim Moloney	7.11	Brian Gilders
18	25-1	Stellar Belle (NZ)	Ivan Tucker	8.9	Bob Skelton
19	25-1	Special Reward	Meggs Elkington	7.7	Billy Smith
20	12-1	Garcon	Tommy Smith	8.6	Des Lake
21	250-1	Blue Special	Russell Wallis	7.11	Bob Durey
22	25-1	Tupaki	Larry Wiggins	7.10	Kevin Langby

Scratched: Terrific, El Gordo, Swift General, Del Charro, Avenium. Won by: Neck, neck. Time: 3:20.4. Track: fast.

Barriers: 15-10-8. Judge's numbers: 5-10-22a.

PATH TO GLORY
Seven starts, two wins, distance covered to the Cup: 11,000 metres

WON	9 ran	8-1	Tony May	9.1	Victoria Park	5 fur	Corporation Hcp	19-Aug-67	Royal Hawa	0:59.3
5TH	12 ran	7-4 fav	Roy Higgins	9.0	Flemington	10 fur	Lord Mayor's Plate	9-Sep-67	Star Belle	2:04.4
3RD	11 ran	3-1	John Miller	8.13	Moonee Valley	10 fur	Glenara Hcp	30-Sep-67	Alcatraz	2:04.1
2ND	15 ran	7-1	Roy Higgins	9.1	Caulfield	8 fur	Toorak Hcp	14-Oct-67	Tobin Bronze	1:36.8
2ND	20 ran	8-1	Roy Higgins	8.8	Caulfield	12 fur	Caulfield Cup	21-Oct-67	Tobin Bronze	2:31.1
4TH	14 ran	15-1	Roy Higgins	9.3	Flemington	10 fur	Mackinnon Stakes	2-Nov-67	Winfreux	2:02.0
WON	22 ran	4-1 ef	Roy Higgins	8.9	Flemington	16 fur	Melbourne Cup	5-Nov-67	Red Crest	3:20.4

 *1974*

THINK BIG

3200 metres (Tuesday, November 5)
Handicap of $150,000 plus trophies valued at $3600.
First: $105,000 plus trophies; Second: $27,000. Third: $12,000. Fourth: $6000.

1	12-1	THINK BIG (NZ)	b g 4y, Sobig (NZ) - Sarcelle (NZ)	Tr: Bart Cummings	53kg	Harry White
2	7-2 fav	LEILANI (NZ)	br m 4y, Oncidium (GB) - Lei (NZ)	Tr: Bart Cummings	55.5kg	Peter Cook
3	14-1	CAPTAIN PERI (NZ)	b g 6y, Della Porta (ITY)- Donna Peri (NZ)	Tr: Jack Wood	52kg	Max Baker

THEN FOLLOWED:

4	20-1	Lord Metric	Merv Ritchie	53	Noel Harris
5	50-1	Piping Lane	Ray Trinder	53	John Stocker
6	7-1	Turfcutter (NZ)	Ray Verner	53	David Peake
7	11-2	Battle Heights (NZ)	Tim Douglas	61	Gary Willetts
8	33-1	Igloo (NZ)	Tommy Smith	57.5	Neville Voigt
9	14-1	Bellota (NZ)	Russell Campbell	51	Stan Aitken
10	20-1	Grand Scale	Maurie Willmott	53	Pat Trotter
11	8-1	Herminia	Des Judd	50	Brian Gilders
12	20-1	Taras Bulba	George Hanlon	47	Lyle Harbridge
13	80-1	Corroboree	Theo Howe	55.5	Darby McCarthy
14	40-1	Passetreul	Tommy Smith	56.5	Kevin Langby
15	200-1	Top Order	Tommy Hughes	43.5	Malcolm Johnston
16	15-1	Gala Supreme	Ray Hutchins	57.5	Frank Reys
17	40-1	Pilfer (NZ)	Colin Hayes	53	John Miller
18	50-1	Gay Master	Tommy Hughes	51	Midge Didham
19	160-1	Our Pocket	Brian Boyle	49.5	John Letts
20	250-1	Sequester	Bob Winks	48	Ray Setches
21	33-1	Big Angel	Eddie Laing	52	Pat Hyland
22	200-1	High Sail (NZ)	Tommy Hughes	53	Alan Cooper

Scratched: Quick Answer, Stop The Music. Won by: 1 length, 1 length. Time: 3:23.2. Track: good.

Barriers: 16-11-17. Judge's numbers: 12-6-15.

PATH TO GLORY
Eight starts, two wins, distance covered to the Cup: 14,750 metres

12TH	14 ran	140-1	Barry Stein	57	Rosehill	1200m	Canterbury Stakes	7-Sep-74	Favoured	1:12.0
10TH	18 ran	20-1	John Duggan	53	Rosehill	2000m	Rosehill Cup	21-Sep-74	Broadway Hit	2:03.6
2ND	11 ran	7-2	Peter Cook	62.5	Rosehill	1850m	Kenthurst Welter	28-Sep-74	Final Verdict	1:56.9
20TH	20 ran	9-1	Peter Cook	53.5	Randwick	2600m	Metropolitan Hcp	7-Oct-74	Passetreul	2:43.3
7TH	13 ran	20-1	Roy Higgins	57	Caulfield	2000m	Coongy Hcp	16-Oct-74	Bellota	2:13.8
8TH	15 ran	25-1	Harry White	54	Moonee Valley	2600m	MV Cup	26-Oct-74	Lord Metric	2:48.0
WON	16 ran	7-1	Harry White	52	Flemington	2500m	Hotham Hcp	2-Nov-74	Gay Master	2:41.1
WON	22 ran	12-1	Harry White	52	Flemington	3200m	Melbourne Cup	5-Nov-74	Leilani	3:23.2

1975

THINK BIG

3200 metres (Tuesday, November 4)
Handicap of $150,000 plus trophies valued at $5600.
First: $105,000 plus trophies. Second: $27,000. Third: $12,000. Fourth: $6000.

1	33-1	THINK BIG (NZ)	b g 5y, Sobig (NZ) - Sarcelle (NZ)	Tr: Bart Cummings	58.5kg	Harry White
2	7-1	HOLIDAY WAGGON (NZ)	ch h 4y, Battle Waggon (GB) - Dolly Gold	Tr: Bart Cummings	50kg	John Duggan
3	125-1	MEDICI	b g 7y, Bourbon Prince (USA)- Azuri (NZ)	Tr: Maurice Hennah	46kg	Malcolm Johnston

THEN FOLLOWED:

4	11-4 fav	Suleiman (NZ)	Bill Winder	52.5	Pat Trotter
5	10-1	Captain Peri (NZ)	Jack Wood	52	John Letts
6	100-1	Sindicato (NZ)	Robert Priscott	53	John Grylls
7	16-1	Turfcutter (NZ)	Ray Verner	52.5	David Peake
8	25-1	Dark Suit	Gary N Hanlon	51	Robert Heffernan
9	40-1	Four Leaf (NZ)	Jim Didham	51	Midge Didham
10	40-1	Chelsea Tower (NZ)	Eric Temperton	54	John Johnston
11	125-1	Calypso	Tommy Smith	51	John Stocker
12	16-1	Guest Star (NZ)	Ivan Tucker	57	Max Baker
13	80-1	Gay Master	Tommy Hughes	53.5	Alan Cooper
14	11-2	Fury's Order (NZ)	Wally McEwan	59.5	Brent Thomson
15	100-1	Comrade Caviar	Les Irwin	47	Alf Matthews
16	20-1	Goodness Knows	Donald Bradfield	46.5	Steven Burridge
17	15-1	Taras Bulba	George Hanlon	57	Gary Willetts
18	25-1	Contere	George Boland	51	Bill Moore
19	50-1	Participator	Tommy Smith	55.5	Kevin Langby
20	10-1	Leica Lover	Bart Cummings	57.5	Roy Higgins

Scratched: Storming, Latin Reign. Won by: 3/4 length, 3 lengths. Time: 3:29.6. Track slow

Barriers: 3-2-13. Judge's numbers: 2-19-22

PATH TO GLORY
Seven starts, one win, distance covered to the Cup: 10,984 metres

6TH	7 ran	250-1	Terry Ryan	58.5	Warwick Farm	1400m	Warwick Stakes	23-Aug-75	Silver Shadow	1:24.8
8TH	8 ran	330-1	Terry Ryan	58	Rosehill	1200m	Canterbury Stakes	6-Sep-75	Leica Show	1:11.6
8TH	15 ran	60-1	Ron Quinton	59	Rosehill	2000m	Rosehill Cup	20-Sep-75	Americano	2:01.8
3RD	5 ran	12-1	Roy Higgins	59	Caulfield	1984m	Caulfield Stakes	11-Oct-75	Guest Star/Zambari	2:08.3
10TH	18 ran	50-1	John Duggan	58.5	Caulfield	2400m	Caulfield Cup	18-Oct-75	Analight	2:30.0
10TH	11 ran	25-1	Harry White	58.5	Flemington	2000m	Mackinnon Stakes	1-Nov-75	Kiwi Can	2:08.3
WON	20 ran	33-1	Harry White	58.5	Flemington	3200m	Melbourne Cup	4-Nov-75	Holiday Waggon	3:29.6

1977

GOLD AND BLACK

3200 metres (Tuesday, November 1)
Handicap of $150,000 plus trophies valued at $6700.
First: $97,500 plus trophies. Second: $30,000. Third: $15,000. Fourth: $7500.

1	7-2 f av	GOLD AND BLACK (NZ)	br g 5y, In The Purple (FR) - Gem (NZ)	Tr: Bart Cummings	57kg	John Duggan
2	11-2	RECKLESS	b/br h 7y, Better Boy (IRE) - Impulsive	Tr: Tom Woodcock	56.5kg	Pat Trotter
3	66-1	HYPERNO (NZ)	b/br g 4y, Rangong (GB) - Mikarla (NZ)	Tr: Geoff Murphy	52kg	Brian Andrews

THEN FOLLOWED:

4	25-1	Gold Pulse	Tommy Smith	51.5	Malcolm Johnston
5	12-1	Unaware	Colin Hayes	55.5	John Stocker
6	50-1	Massuk	Jim Houlahan	48	Alan Trevena
7	33-1	Valadero	Tommy Hughes	54	Midge Didham
8	20-1	Ming Dynasty	Bart Cummings	56	Harry White
9	30-1	Trochee (NZ)	Peter McLean	51	Bill Skelton
10	33-1	Van Der Hum (NZ)	Leo Robinson	58	Bob Skelton
11	66-1	Royal Cadenza	Stuart Dromgool	57	Roger Lang
12	7-1	Salamander	Tommy Hughes	54.5	Roy Higgins
13	10-1	Major Till	Colin Hayes	51	Mick Mallyon
14	20-1	Yashmak	Mick Robins	51	John Letts
15	12-1	Brallos	Philip Banham	52.5	Max Baker
16	160-1	Wave King	Jim Hely	52	Darby McCarthy
17	25-1	Family Of Man	George Hanlon	54.5	Brent Thomson
18	20-1	Happy Union (NZ)	Bill Winder	55.5	Pat Hyland
19	125-1	Grey Affair	Jim Atkins	52	Gary Palmer
20	50-1	Vacuum	Bart Cummings	53	Wayne Treloar
21	33-1	Shaitan (NZ)	Bill Sanders	55.5	Ron Taylor
22	14-1	Sir Serene	Tommy Smith	53	Peter Cook
23	200-1	Beau's Demand (NZ)	Ron McDonell	51	Robert Heffernan
24	200-1	Peteken (NZ)	WP Roche	52	Gary Willetts

All started. Won by: 1 length, 2-1/2 lengths. Time: 3:18.4. Track: fast.

Barriers: 14-16-3. Judge's numbers: 2-4-16.

PATH TO GLORY
Eight starts, one win, distance covered to the Cup: 12,600 metres.

17TH	17 ran	250-1	Michael Domingo	58	Morphettville	1000m	Wylie Stakes	20-Aug-77	Bonfield	56.7
6TH	8 ran	40-1	Alan Trevena	58.5	Caulfield	1600m	Memsie Stakes	3-Sep-77	Wave King	1:39.8
10TH	10 ran	40-1	Alan Trevena	58.5	Flemington	1600m	Craiglee Stakes	10-Sep-77	Ming Dynasty	1:38.0
5TH	11 ran	66-1	John Duggan	59	Caulfield	2000m	Underwood Stakes	22-Sep-77	Denise's Joy	2:00.8
8TH	11 ran	16-1	Wayne Treloar	59	Caulfield	2000m	Caulfield Stakes	8-Oct-77	Family Of Man	2:00.7
5TH	18 ran	25-1	John Duggan	57	Caulfield	2400m	Caulfield Cup	15-Oct-77	Ming Dynasty	2:28.5
2ND	10 ran	12-1	John Duggan	59	Flemington	2000m	Mackinnon Stakes	29-Oct-77	Sir Silver Lad	2:02.4
WON	24 ran	7-2 fav	John Duggan	57	Flemington	3200m	Melbourne Cup	1-Nov-77	Reckless	3:18.4

1979

HYPERNO

3200 metres (Tuesday, November 6)
Handicap of $300,000 plus trophies valued at $10,000.
First: $195,000 plus trophies; Second: $60,000. Third: $30,000. Fourth: $15,000.

1	7-1	HYPERNO (NZ)	b/br g 6y, Rangong (GB) - Mikaria (NZ)	Tr: Bart Cummings	56kg	Harry White
2	10-1	SALAMANDER	b g 6y, Approval (GB) - Sister Eve	Tr: Tommy Hughes	55.5kg	Roy Higgins
3	16-1	RED NOSE (NZ)	b g 4y, Reindeer (IRE) - Pin (NZ)	Tr: Theo Green	51.5kg	Midge Didham

THEN FOLLOWED:

4	40-1	Hauberk	Bob Hoysted	51	Paul Jarman
5	13-2	Cubacade (NZ)	Don Couchman	52	Jim Walker
6	6-1	Warri Symbol	Jim Moloney	52	Pat Hyland
7	12-1	Karu (NZ)	Jack Holmes	49	Warwick Robinson
8	16-1	Magistrate	Ian Steffert	51.5	Bob Skelton
9	50-1	Kankama (NZ)	Mark Sullivan	54	John Stocker
10	25-1	Earthquake McGoon	Geoff Murphy	51	Gary Willetts
11	66-1	Sarfraz (NZ)	Jim Moloney	50.5	Alan Trevena
12	20-1	Pigalle (NZ)	Geoff Murphy	47.5	Brendan Clements
13	40-1	Love Bandit	Tommy Hughes	48.5	Gary Palmer
14	200-1	Jessephenie	Len Dixon	47	Steven Burridge
15	50-1	Somerset Nile	Chris Honeychurch	50	Ray Selkrig
16	100-1	Over The Ocean (NZ)	Tommy Smith	51	Wayne Treloar
17	33-1	Iko	Tommy Smith	49.5	Malcolm Johnston
18	80-1	Gunderman	Theo Howe	51.5	Robertt Heffernan
19	160-1	Licence Fee (NZ)	Tommy Harrison	49.5	Alan Williams
20	66-1	Rough 'N' Tough (NZ)	Terry Millard	52	Garry Murphy
21	100-1	Safe Harbour	Bart Cummings	49.5	Kevin Langby
PU	3-1 fav	Dulcify (NZ)	Colin Hayes	56	Brent Thomson

Scratched: Panamint, Pierree's Order. Won by: short 1/2 head, 1-3/4 lengths. Time: 3:21.8. Track: fast.

Barriers: 11-2-3. Judge's numbers: 2-4-12.

PATH TO GLORY
Seven starts, one win, distance covered to the Cup: 10,600 metres.

14TH	14 ran	15-1	Roy Higgins	57.5	Flemington	1000m	Aurie's Star Hcp	29-Aug-79	Mellow Tint	58.3
10TH	15 ran	16-1	Roy Higgins	58.5	Flemington	1600m	Craiglee Stakes	8-Sep-79	Dulcify	1:37.6
5TH	13 ran	5-1	Gary Willetts	58.5	Flemington	1400m	Wiridigil Hcp	9-Oct-79	Consenting	1:25.9
5TH	14 ran	20-1	Brent Thomson	59	Caulfield	2000m	Caulfield Stakes	13-Oct-79	Mighty Kingdom	2:04.6
6TH	13 ran	9-4 fav	Roy Higgins	57	Moonee Valley	2600m	Governor's Stakes	27-Oct-79	Sir Sahib	2:44.9
4TH	10 ran	33-1	Harry White	59	Flemington	2000m	Mackinnon Stakes	3-Nov-79	Dulcify	2:00.9
WON	22 ran	7-1	Harry White	56	Flemington	3200m	Melbourne Cup	6-Nov-79	Salamander	3:21.8

1990

KINGSTON RULE

3200 metres (Tuesday, November 6)
Handicap of $2,000,000 plus trophies valued at $35,000.
First: $1,300,000 plus trophies; Second: $400,000. Third: $200,000. Fourth: $100,000.

1	7-1 eq fav	KINGSTON RULE (USA)	(ch h 5y, Secretariat (USA) - Rose Of Kingston)	Tr: Bart Cummings	53kg	Darren Beadman
2	7-1 eq fav	THE PHANTOM (NZ)	(b g 5y, Noble Bijou (USA) - The Fantasy (NZ)	Tr: Murray Baker	54.5kg	Grant Cooksley
3	14-1	MR. BROOKER (NZ)	(b g 5y, Our Best Friend (USA) - Astro Hit)	Tr: Peter Hurdle	53kg	Greg Childs

THEN FOLLOWED:

4	33-1	Na Botto (NZ)	Peter Hollinshead	50.5	Larry Cassidy
5	20-1	Mount Olympus	David Hayes	48.5	Michael Carson
6	40-1	Aquidity (NZ)	Sue Walsh	54.5	David Walsh
7	66-1	Savage Toss (ARG)	Lee Freedman	57	Brian Hibberd
8	10-1	Flying Luskin	Trevor McKee	55	Peter Johnson
9	33-1	La Tristia (NZ)	Bart Cummings	48.5	Steven King
10	33-1	Our Magic Man (NZ)	Jim Lee	49	Kevin Moses
11	16-1	Sydeston	Bob Hoysted	58.5	Mick Dittman
12	12-1	Just A Dancer (NZ)	Graeme Rogerson	51	Jim Cassidy
13	14-1	Chaleyer	Frank Lewis	50.5	Shane Dye
14	11-1	Ali Boy (NZ)	Mark Phillips	50.5	Harry White
15	10-1	Shuzohra (NZ)	Errol Skelton	53	Larry Olsen
16	25-1	Tawriffic (NZ)	Lee Freedman	56.5	Darren Gauci
17	33-1	Rainbow Myth (NZ)	Ralph Manning	51.5	Michael Clarke
18	250-1	Dalraffin	Bede Murray	50.5	Kevin Forrester
19	10-1	Water Boatman (IRE)	David Hayes	55	Peter Hutchinson
20	25-1	Frontier Boy (NZ)	Lee Freedman	51	Damien Oliver
21	140-1	Betoota (NZ)	Wayne Walters	50	Robert Heffernan
22	330-1	Rising Fear	Larry Pickering	48.5	Colin Browell
23	100-1	Selwyn's Mate (NZ)	Michael Moroney	49	Brian Werner
24	50-1	Donegal Mist (NZ)	Geoff Maynes	50.5	John Marshall

All started. Won by: 1 length, neck. Time: 3:16.3 (Track record). Track: fast

Barriers: 1-5-22. Judge's numbers: 8-7-9.

PATH TO GLORY
Eight starts, two wins, distance covered to the Cup: 13,423 metres.

8TH	12 ran	4-1	Len Maund	57.5	Moonee Valley	1223m	5yo+ Hcp	8-Aug-90	Princess Pushy	1:16.3
5TH	12 ran	16-1	Len Maund	58.5	Caulfield	1400m	Memsie Stakes	1-Sep-90	The Phantom	1:25.6
4TH	16 ran	7-1	Len Maund	58.5	Flemington	1600m	Craiglee Stakes	8-Sep-90	Zabeel	1:36.5
8TH	16 ran	6-4 fav	Len Maund	55	Sandown	2100m	Open Hcp	22-Sep-90	Imperial Salute	2:09.3
2ND	12 ran	9-2	Jim Cassidy	53	Caulfield	a2000m	Coongy Hcp	17-Oct-90	Kessem	2:00.6
WON	15 ran	4-1 fav	Jim Cassidy	53	Moonee Valley	2600m	Moonee Valley Cup	27-Oct-90	Flying Luskin	2:40.1
2ND	13 ran	11-2	Darren Beadman	56	Flemington	2500m	The Dalgety	3-Nov-90	Mount Olympus	2:33.6
WON	24 ran	7-1 fav	Darren Beadman	53	Flemington	3200m	Melbourne Cup	6-Nov-90	The Phantom	3:16.3

1991

LET'S ELOPE

3200 metres (Tuesday, November 5)
Group 1. Handicap of $2,000,000 plus trophies valued at $35,000.
First: $1,300,000 plus trophies; Second: $400,000. Third: $200,000. Fourth: $100,000

1	3-1 fav	LET'S ELOPE (NZ)	(ch m 4y. Nassipour (USA) - Sharon Jane (NZ)	Tr: Bart Cummings	51kg	Steven King
2	10-1	SHIVA'S REVENGE (NZ)	(b g 4y, Nassipour (USA) - How About Now)	Tr: Bart Cummings	53.5kg	Shane Dye
3	50-1	MAGNOLIA HALL (NZ)	(ch g 5y, Noble Bijou (USA) - Gone With The Wind (NZ)	Tr: Helen Page	52.5kg	Brian York

THEN FOLLOWED:

4	20-1	Super Impose (NZ)	Lee Freedman	60	Darren Beadman
5	6-1	Ivory Way (USA)	David Hayes	49.5	Michael Clarke
6	25-1	Rasheek (USA)	David Hayes	51.5	Peter Hutchinson
7	16-1	Al Maheb (USA)	David Hayes	56.5	Darren Gauci
8	14-1	Just A Dancer (NZ)	Graeme Rogerson	56.5	Jim Cassidy
9	8-1	Castletown (NZ)	Paddy Busuttin	57	Noel Harris
10	40-1	Grooming	Lee Freedman	51.5	Damien Oliver
11	50-1	Maharajah (NZ)	Tommy Smith	49.5	Malcolm Johnston
12	80-1	Moods	Alf Marshall	49.5	Bruce Compton
13	14-1	Lord Revenir (NZ)	Bruce Wallace	54	Grant Cooksley
14	33-1	Sydeston	Bob Hoysted	57.5	Mick Dittman
15	100-1	Cool Credit	George Hanlon	50.5	Kevin Forrester
16	40-1	Alphabel (IRE)	David Hayes	53	Glen Darrington
17	16-1	Diego (NZ)	Dave O'Sullivan	52.5	Lance O'Sullivan
18	14-1	Te Akau Pearl (NZ)	Michael Moroney	50	Jim Collett
19	33-1	Nayrizi (Ire.)	Pat Hyland	54	Greg Hall
20	40-1	Dr. Grace (NZ)	Geoff Chapman	56	Kevin Moses
21	100-1	Pontiac Lass (NZ)	Murray Baker	49.5	Tony Allan
22	50-1	Weekend Delight (NZ)	Bart Cummings	50.5	Greg Childs
23	125-1	Rural Prince (NZ)	Graham Sanders	49.5	Larry Cassidy
24	330-1	Sunshine Sally	George Hanlon	48	Patrick Payne

All started. Won by: 2-1/2 lengths, head. Time: 3:18.9. Track: fast. #Protest: 2nd against 1st dismissed.

Barriers: 10-4-18. Judge's numbers: 15-9-12.

PATH TO GLORY

Seven starts, four wins, distance covered to the Cup: 10,800 metres.

4TH	18 ran	50-1	Glen Darrington	51.5	Caulfield	1200m	Open Hcp	7-Sep-91	Impoteric	1:12.6
3RD	16 ran	14-1	Simon Marshall	55	Flemington	1400m	Milady Stakes	14-Sept-91	Shavano Miss	1:25.5
10TH	12 ran	11-4 fav	Shane Dye	52	Caulfield	1800m	Royal Show Hcp	26-Sep-91	Newbury Star	1:53.6
WON	13 ran	7-1	Steven King	50	Flemington	2000m	Turnbull Stakes	5-Oct-91	Prince Salieri	2:01.9
WON	18 ran	7-1	Steven King	48.5	Caulfield	2400m	Caulfield Cup	19-Oct-91	Ivory Way	2:30.3
WON	13 ran	7-1	Steven King	54.5	Flemington	2000m	Mackinnon Stakes	2-Nov-91	Super Impose	2:01.8
WON	24 ran	3-1 fav	Steven King	51	Flemington	3200m	Melbourne Cup	5-Nov-91	Shiva's Revenge	3:18.9

1996

SAINTLY

3200 metres (Tuesday, November 5)

Group 1. Handicap of $2,200,000 and $35,000 trophies. First: $1,430,000 and Gold Cup of $32,500 to owner, miniature Gold Cups of $1000 each to trainer and jockey and for the strapper the Tommy Woodcock trophy of $500 value. Second: $440,000. Third: $198,000; Fourth: $88,000; Fifth: $44,000.

1	8-1	SAINTLY	ch g 4y. Sky Chase (NZ) - All Grace (NZ)	Tr: Bart Cummings	55.5kg	Darren Beadman
2	33-1	COUNT CHIVAS (NZ)	b g 5y. Lord Ballina - Inquisit (NZ)	Tr: Lee Freedman	57kg	Steven King
3	50-1	SKYBEAU (NZ)	b g 4y. Dahar (USA) - Beaumont Babe	Tr: Len Smith	50kg	Jason Holder

THEN FOLLOWED:

4	10-1	Senator (NZ)	Jack Tims	53		Lance O'Sullivan
5	7-1	Nothin' Leica Dane	Gai Waterhouse	55		Shane Dye
6	13-2	Doriemus (NZ)	Lee Freedman	58		Damien Oliver
7	25-1	Grey Shot (GB)	Ian Balding	55		Pat Eddery
8	66-1	Sapio (NZ)	Sylvia Kay	54		Jim Walker
9	66-1	Alcove	Tommy Hughes jr	50		Brian York
10	66-1	Cheviot	Cliff Brown	50.5		Damian Browne
11	15-1	The Bandette (NZ)	John Wheeler	51		Noel Harris
12	14-1	Arctic Scent	Jim Mason	51.5		Brent Stanley
13	15-1	Istidaad (USA)	Peter Hayes	53.5		Greg Hall
14	16-1	Circles Of Gold	Brian Smith	50.5		Brett Prebble
15	4-1 fav	Oscar Schindler (IRE)	Kevin Prendergast	56.5		Mick Kinane
16	125-1	Centico (NZ)	John Sadler	48.5		Andrew Payne
17	125-1	The Phantom Chance (NZ)	John Wheeler	53.5		Patrick Payne
18	50-1	Super Slew	Clarry Conners	51.5		Mick Dittman
19	33-1	Few Are Chosen	Gai Waterhouse	50.5		Darren Gauci
20	25-1	Court Of Honour (IRE)	Peter Chapple-Hyam	56.5		Simon Marshall
21	33-1	My Kiwi Gold (NZ)	Bart Cummings	49.5		John Marshall
22	50-1	Beaux Art	David Edwards	52		Jeremy Hustwitt

Scratched: Crying Game, Magnet Bay. Won by: 2-1/4 length, neck. Time: 3:18.8. Track: good.

Barriers: 3-13-7. Judge's numbers: 5-2-22.

PATH TO GLORY
Seven starts, three wins, distance covered to the Cup: 11,540 metres.

2ND	8 ran	6-4 fav	Darren Beadman	57	Warwick Farm	1400m	Warwick Stakes	25-Aug-96	Filante	1:21.7
2ND	11 ran	2-1	Darren Beadman	57	Randwick	1600m	Chelmsford Stakes	7-Sep-96	Filante	1:35.0
WON	10 ran	9-10 fav	Darren Beadman	57	Rosehill	1900m	Hill Stakes	21-Sep-96	Nothin'Leica Dane	1:56.2
2ND	8 ran	1-3 fav	Darren Beadman	57	Randwick	2000m	Craven Plate	5-Oct-96	Adventurous	2:02.0
3RD	14 ran	1-1 fav	Darren Beadman	54.5	Randwick	2600m	Metropolitan Hcp	7-Oct-96	Hula Flight	2:44.3
WON	8 ran	5-1	Darren Beadman	57	Moonee Valley	2040m	W S Cox Plate	26-Oct-96	Filante	2:05.7
WON	22 ran	8-1	Darren Beadman	55.5	Flemington	3200m	Melbourne Cup	5-Nov-96	Count Chivas	3:18.8

 *1999*

ROGAN JOSH

3200 metres (Tuesday, November 2)
Group 1. Handicap. of $3,000,000 and $35,000 trophies. First: $1,800,000 plus trophies; Second: $480,000; Third: $225,000; Fourth: $115,000; Fifth: $80,000. Sixth to 10th: $60,000.

1	5-1	ROGAN JOSH	b g 7y, Old Spice - Eastern Mystique	Tr: Bart Cummings	50lg	John Marshall
2	50-1	CENTRAL PARK (IRE)	ch h 5y, In The Wings (GB) - Park Special (IRE)	Tr: Saeed Bin Suroor	57.5kg	Frankie Dettori
=3	140-1	LAHAR	gr m 5y, Kenmare (FR) - Volcanic (NZ)	Tr: Paul Cave	50.5kg	Corey Brown
=3	50-1	ZAZABELLE (NZ)	b m 4y, Zabeel (NZ) - The Perfume Garden (NZ)	Tr: Bart Cummings	49kg	Eddie Wilkinson

THEN FOLLOWED:

5	9-1	Travelmate (GB)	Jamie Fanshawe	52.5	David Harrison
6	50-1	The Warrior (NZ)	Richard Otto	49	Gary Grylls
7	60-1	Second Coming (NZ)	Michael Moroney	51	Greg Childs
8	11-1	The Hind (NZ)	Peter Hayes	52.5	Jim Cassidy
9	20-1	Bohemiath	John Sadler	50	Jason Patton
10	40-1	Brew (NZ)	Michael Moroney	49	Lance O'Sullivan
11	250-1	Zabuan (NZ)	Jim Moloney	49	Sam Hyland
12	30-1	Yavana's Pace (IRE)	Mark Johnston	53.5	Richard Hughes
13	16-1	Streak	Robert Smerdon	51.5	Greg Hall
14	7-1	Tie The Knot	Guy Walter	58	Shane Dye
15	160-1	Figurehead (NZ)	Kay Lane	50.5	Opie Bosson
16	66-1	Skybeau (NZ)	Len Smith	52	Larry Cassidy
17	7-2 fav	Sky Heights (NZ)	Colin Alderson	56.5	Damien Oliver
18	66-1	Lady Elsie	Cliff Brown	49.5	Len Beasley
19	10-1	Laebeel (NZ)	John Sadler	49.5	Stephen Baster
20	66-1	Maridpour (IRE)	Michael Moroney	55	Steven Arnold
21	200-1	The Message (NZ)	John Ralph	52	Aaron Spiteri
22	15-1	Arena	John Hawkes	54.5	Darren Gauci
23	66-1	Rebbor (NZ)	Bart Cummings	49	Chris Munce
LR	50-1	Able Master (NZ)	Bruce Wallace	50.5	Grant Cooksley

All started. Won by: 1/2 length, 1/2 neck. Time: 3:19.6. Track: good.

Barriers: 21-19-8 (Lahar) 13 (Zazabelle). Judge's numbers: 17-2-12/14.

PATH TO GLORY
Seven starts, three wins, distance covered to the Cup: 11,640 metres.

7TH	7 ran	8-1	Brett Prebble	56.5	Flemington	1200m	Open Hcp	25-Aug-99	Hula Wonder	1:10.18
10TH	15 ran	70-1	Patrick Payne	58	Moonee Valley	1600m	JF Feehan Stakes	11-Sep-99	Inaflury	1:40.02
7TH	14 ran	12-1	Patrick Payne	55	Moonee Valley	2040m	JRA Cup	23-Sep-99	Brave Chief	2:05.60
WON	11 ran	12-1	Darren Gauci	53	Caulfield	2400m	Perrier Stakes	9-Oct-99	The Hind	2:27.63
4TH	18 ran	25-1	Chris Munce	51.5	Caulfield	2400m	Caulfield Cup	16-Oct-99	Sky Heights	2:30.10
WON	13 ran	16-1	John Marshall	58	Flemington	2000m	Mackinnon Stakes	30-Oct-99	Rebel	2:00.34
WON	24 ran	5-1	John Marshall	50	Flemington	3200m	Melbourne Cup	2-Nov-99	Central Park	3:19.64

2008

VIEWED

3200 metres (Tuesday, November 4)
Group 1. Handicap of $5,500,000 plus $150,000 trophies. First: $330,000 plus trophies; Second: $835,000;
Third: $420,000; Fourth: $220,000; Fifth: $150,000; Sixth to 10th: $115,000.

1	$41.00	VIEWED	b g 5y Scenic (IRE) - Lovers Knot (NZ)	Tr: Bart Cummings	53kg	Blake Shinn
2	$21.00	BAUER (IRE)	gr h 6y, Halling (USA) - Dali's Grey (GB)	Tr: Luca Cumani	52kg	Corey Brown
3	$21.00	C'EST LA GUERRE (NZ)	b g 4y, Shinko King (IRE) - La Magnifique (NZ)	Tr: John Sadler	54kg	Brett Prebble

THEN FOLLOWED:

4	26.00	Master O'Reilly (NZ)	Danny O'Brien	55	Vlad Duric
5	9.00	Profound Beauty (Ire.)	Dermot Weld	51.5	Glen Boss
6	31.00	Moatize	Bart Cummings	50	Clare Lindop
7	5.50 fav	Mad Rush (USA)	Luca Cumani	53.5	Damien Oliver
8	7.50	Nom Du Jeu (NZ)	Murray Baker	54	Jeff Lloyd
9	15.00	Zipping	John Sadler	54	Danny Nikolic
10	61.00	Newport	Paul Perry	51.5	Chris Symons
11	51.00	Ice Chariot	Ron Maund	53	Michael Rodd
12	151.00	Guyno (NZ)	Lou Luciani	52	Craig Newitt
13	31.00	Littorio	Nigel Blackiston	52.5	Steven King
14	101.00	Varevees (GB)	Richard Gibson	51.5	Craig Williams
15	81.00	Boundless (NZ)	Stephen McKee	52	Greg Childs
16	101.00	Red Lord	Anthony Cummings	51.5	Nicholas Hall (a)
17	61.00	Prize Lady (NZ)	Graeme Sanders	51	Mark Sweeney
18	7.00	Septimus (Ire.)	Aidan O'Brien	58.5	John Murtagh
19	16.00	Barbaricus	Danny O'Brien	50.5	Stephen Baster
20	41.00	Alessandro Volta (GB)	Aidan O'Brien	50.5	Wayne Lordan
21	21.00	Honolulu (Ire.)	Aidan O'Brien	54.5	Colm O'Donoghue
PU	31.00	Gallopin (NZ)	Danny O'Brien	52	James Winks

Scratched: Yellowstone, Zarita. Won by: Nose, 2 lengths. Time: 3:20.40. (Last 600m 34.93). Track: good (3).

Barriers: 8-11-5. Judge's numbers: 10-12-4-2.

PATH TO GLORY

Five starts (raced in June in Brisbane), one win, distance covered to the Cup: 7600 metres.

8TH	15 ran	$10	Michael Rodd	58	Flemington	1400m	HKJC Stakes	6-Sep-08	Stavka	1:23.2
7TH	13 ran	$51	Damien Oliver	59	Caulfield	1800m	Underwood Stakes	20-Sep-08	Weekend Hussler	1:49.8
10TH	17 ran	$41	Blake Shinn	54.5	Caulfield	2400m	Caulfield Cup	18-Oct-08	All The Good	2:27.4
11TH	11 ran	$6	Steven Arnold	59	Flemington	2000m	Mackinnon Stakes	1-Nov-08	Theseo	2:03.8
WON	22 ran	$41	Blake Shinn	53	Flemington	3200m	Melbourne Cup	4-Nov-08	Bauer	3:20.4

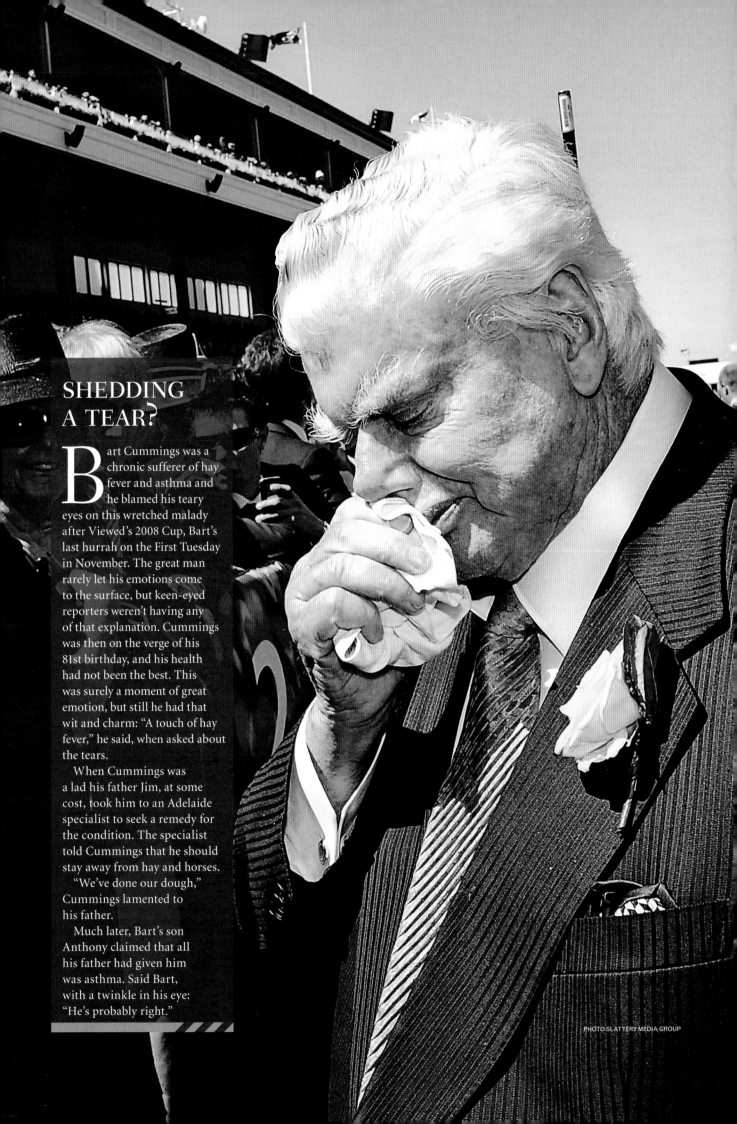

SHEDDING A TEAR?

Bart Cummings was a chronic sufferer of hay fever and asthma and he blamed his teary eyes on this wretched malady after Viewed's 2008 Cup, Bart's last hurrah on the First Tuesday in November. The great man rarely let his emotions come to the surface, but keen-eyed reporters weren't having any of that explanation. Cummings was then on the verge of his 81st birthday, and his health had not been the best. This was surely a moment of great emotion, but still he had that wit and charm: "A touch of hay fever," he said, when asked about the tears.

When Cummings was a lad his father Jim, at some cost, took him to an Adelaide specialist to seek a remedy for the condition. The specialist told Cummings that he should stay away from hay and horses.

"We've done our dough," Cummings lamented to his father.

Much later, Bart's son Anthony claimed that all his father had given him was asthma. Said Bart, with a twinkle in his eye: "He's probably right."